"Annelie Rozeboom sp   ...nomads, civil servants, farmers, intellectuals, monks, refugees, aid workers, rich and poor, oppressed and oppressors, and with the Dalai Lama himself. A masterpiece, considering the restrictions the Chinese imposed on her and the hesitancy of the Tibetans." – *Volkskrant*

"Rozeboom, former correspondent in Beijing, visited this fascinating region, but without dwelling on its mysticism. ... Little by little it becomes clear what a complicated and divided country Tibet is." – *Trouw*

"An interesting book with two important qualities: thematic diversity and lots of attention to eyewitness accounts of people who were really there." – *Bibnet*

Waiting for the Dalai Lama

Stories from all sides of the Tibetan debate

Annelie Rozeboom

BLACKSMITH BOOKS

Waiting for the Dalai Lama

ISBN 978-988-17742-0-0

Published by Blacksmith Books
5th Floor, 24 Hollywood Road,
Central, Hong Kong
Tel: (+852) 2877 7899
www.blacksmithbooks.com

Contents

INTRODUCTION

PICTURES OF THE DALAI LAMA

The old woman in front of the Jokhang temple shows two brown teeth. She mutters incomprehensibly and holds out her hand. Another beggar, I think. In Lhasa they follow you around; kids with home-made wooden musical instruments which they play for two seconds before asking for money; monks with a plastic bag full of change who want a contribution for their monastery, and now this old woman in front of the temple. Behind us, pilgrims throw themselves to the ground. First, they stand upright, hands crossed on their chests, and muttering prayers. Then they let themselves drop like planks. Their hands land on small rectangular pieces of cardboard, which slide forward producing scraping noises as their bodies fall.

I sigh and find an old five-mao note in my bag. According to the *Lonely Planet*, this is the acceptable amount. "Give just as much as the locals," was the stern warning. "You don't want beggars to think that Westerners give more." But when I stuff the dirty note into her hand, the woman gives me a bewildered look. What am I doing wrong, I ask myself. Not enough? Has there been inflation? Then a man next to me starts laughing. "She asked you for a picture of the Dalai Lama and you gave her money," he chuckles.

Have I started thinking like a Chinese? They also seem to be convinced that the Tibetans want money, while many of them just want their religious leader back. The day before my visit to the temple I listened to a monologue from a very nice, albeit rather boring, Chinese official working in Lhasa. It took him three hours to explain to me that Tibetans want riches and development. "It's like that everywhere in the world and there is absolutely no reason why this would be different in Tibet," he said.

He was partly right, I discovered. Of course the Tibetans want to develop. But they are also deeply religious, and if they had to choose between their faith and the Chinese plans for development, the Chinese wouldn't stand a chance. The big problem is that the Tibetans were never given a choice. Ever since 1950, the year that the Chinese army invaded Tibet, the Chinese Communist Party has promised development. The Chinese built roads and schools. The leaders from Beijing claim to have invested three billion dollars in the 'Autonomous Region' over the last 30 years. According to the Chinese press, this investment has paid off and Tibetan GDP has increased tenfold.

In exchange the Tibetans gave up their independence and their cultural and religious traditions. The Chinese called this "the people's liberation from feudal monasteries and rich landowners." The region, which until then had been closed to foreigners, was governed by a religious and political leader, the Dalai Lama. After the invasion, the Dalai Lama tried to work together with the aggressors from Beijing. He sent a delegation, but the representatives were forced to sign a '17-point agreement'. The document stipulated that Tibet from now on would be part of China, but Mao Zedong also promised the Tibetans their freedom of religion and self-government.

It didn't take long, however, before the Chinese authorities started to breach the conditions of their own agreement. When rumors started going around that the authorities were planning to kidnap the Dalai Lama, the religious leader fled to India. Eighty thousand followers decided to go with him. Together, they started a refugee community and a government in exile. Tibet's second in command, the Panchen Lama, stayed behind.

He tried to collaborate with the new authorities and ended up in jail. Then, in the 1960s, the Chinese brought their Cultural Revolution to Tibet. Thousands of monasteries and temples were destroyed. A million Tibetans lost their lives. Not all Tibetans fared badly. Former slaves and farmers, who used to be owned by royal families and monasteries, were given the land on which they had been forced to work for generations. Hundreds of beggars, nomads and poor farmers were sent to school in Chinese provinces and were given jobs as government officials. Some of them became China's most faithful supporters. When their leaders talk about the Dalai Lama and his followers, they talk about "those separatist terrorists".

In Tibet itself, however, it's hard to find such a harsh opinion of the religious leader-in-exile. Simple farmers and nomads say that they hope their Dalai Lama will return. They don't like it that they're not allowed to keep his picture. These portraits are, of course, available on the black market; like all rules and laws in China, this one is also implemented with amazing inconsistency. The locals also know that Westerners will give you a free portrait. You just stick out your hand to one of these blond devils, and out comes a Dalai Lama picture. They are right, too. There are lots of tourists who give away the much wanted photos and even the biography of the Dalai Lama. Now that I know, I notice that everywhere I go people yell some version of "Dalai Lama picture" at me. Even the nomad kids, whom we encounter by the side of the road outside Lhasa, want candy and a picture. When I tell them that I have neither, they try to open my bag. They don't believe me. What else would I be carrying around?

Despite the promises of the Chinese government, economic development in Tibet has been slow, especially if you compare it to the incredible growth that has taken place in the rest of China. When China started to liberalize its policies in the 1980s, there seemed some hope for Tibet. The monasteries were allowed to open. Then party secretary Hu Yaobang visited Tibet and he stated that he was appalled by the poverty.

He promised to set things straight as fast as he could. But the liberal Hu Yaobang didn't stay in power long enough. He was toppled and, instead of liberalization, another round of political crackdowns followed. At the end of the eighties, monks and nuns organized a series of demonstrations for their independence. The Chinese sent the army and the soldiers shot at demonstrators and the public alike. Many people were arrested. The tourists, who had just discovered Tibet, were thrown out and the region was closed once again. And history keeps repeating itself. After a decade of relative calm, new riots in Tibet hit the headlines in the run-up to the Olympic Games in Beijing in 2008. The exiled Tibetan leaders say 203 people died in the riots and subsequent government crackdown. China accused "rioters" of being responsible for 21 deaths.

The Chinese blame the "separatists" for the economic underdevelopment of the region. They still promise a Tibet free of poverty in the next few decades, if only those monks would stop demonstrating. The "separatists", on the other hand, declare that the Chinese are the only people who profit from any economic development in Tibet. In the beginning, they say, the Chinese built roads because the army needed to send its trucks. Now it's the Chinese immigrants who run all the new restaurants and who build the new buildings. Because of this, it's very difficult to help economic development in Tibet. Foreign governments set up projects to help Tibetans, only to discover a few months later that hundreds of Chinese laborers are imported from neighboring provinces to do all the work. ·

The Tibetans will never stop opposing the Chinese presence in their country, they say. They feel oppressed by a group of very bad people. They are also scared. In Tibet, people don't start talking about the Dalai Lama by themselves. If they say anything about him in the following interviews, it's because I specifically asked them. I wasn't looking for political views, though. I was much more fascinated by the unimaginably long roads these people had traveled during their lifetimes. From their upbringing in isolated villages in one of the remotest places in the world, to adult lives as a unique group of people who have discovered the world around them, whatever side they are on now, the arrival of the Chinese army changed their lives forever. Not because they wanted it to, but because history washed over them.

I shared the idea of writing this book with Iliana, a French journalist with whom I lived in an apartment in Beijing. She brought the first Living Buddha – according to the Tibetans, someone who has, after going though all stages of reincarnation, obtained the spiritual level of a Buddha – into our house. He had lived in Switzerland for 20 years and spoke about five words of German. Now he was back in his hometown. The Dutch embassy funded a clinic for traditional medicine in his place in eastern Tibet. He needed to go see his sponsors, he said. Could I please go with him? He wanted to ask for money for a car to transport sick people, and his Buddha statues needed a new coat of gold. I arranged a meeting. The Living Buddha put on his traditional coat, took a bunch of white shawls and we went to ask for funds. The Dutch diplomats were very friendly. They politely draped the white shawls around their necks. After the visit to the embassy, the Living Buddha asked me to take him to the disco. We went home, where he exchanged his nomad coat for a modern suit and we had a great time on the dancefloor.

The next Tibetan who came was a scholar who worked in Beijing for a Tibetan research institute. He was married. Iliana soon found herself trapped in the same hopeless situation that almost every woman who dates a married man ends up in. He promised to divorce; his marriage had been arranged anyway. This never happened. Iliana gave English lessons to his 16-year-old son. When she, in a burst of emotion, gave the son enough money to escape to India, the whole family went on a nice holiday to Tibet and duly came back a few weeks later.

The father wanted Iliana to write a book about his life. This had to be done in utter secrecy. I'm not sure why, because the book was very pro-

China. It was the life story of a poor slave who had been educated by the Chinese. There was not one word of criticism in it. But it did give us the idea to report the different life stories of Tibetan people.

Iliana had sources enough. The next boyfriend was a Tibetan salesman from Chengdu, a provincial Chinese town bordering Tibet. He hated the Chinese and even refused to sit in the same room with one. He sold tangkas, religious paintings on silk. Iliana spent two thousand dollars on them and thought she could sell them at enormous profits in Beijing. It turned out that her prices were a bit over the top. However, I liked Tashi, the merchant. He stayed and tried to help her when she succumbed to drugs and alcohol abuse. In the end, she packed her bags and disappeared to Tibet, Nepal, India. Instead of writing the biographies of Tibetans, she went to study Buddhism. I don't know where she is now, but in the regions around Tibet I have met many lost souls like her, people who don't know what they are looking for. Some of them find a home in a Buddhist monastery or as a volunteer among the friendly Tibetan refugees.

All this had roused my curiosity about Tibet. I had lived in China for ten years, and knew all about the good and the bad sides of the Chinese. I know that the Chinese people are not a group of terrible monsters, as they are sometimes depicted by pro-Tibet activists. And the Tibetans I had met did not match the sacred-monk image that they are sometimes given in the Western press.

The Chinese are fascinating people, idealists at times, but after all their revolutions, mostly demoralized. They are also very proud, a people that longs for the greatness of long-gone imperial dynasties. Respect for the individual is not part of the culture. The idea that one should help the poor is also quite new in China. Instead, the Chinese tend to look down on anybody who has less than they have. Chinese farmers suffer from this greatly. When a farmer comes to the city – and they come in their millions – they are treated badly. This superiority complex gets even worse when city people meet members of what they call their national minorities. One of my teachers at Peking University, the most prestigious educational institution in China, described the Tibetans to us, his students, as follows: "They are barbarians. They are very dirty. They wear these thick coats that never get washed. When they eat their huge pieces of fried mutton, the oil just drips down these disgusting coats." There's racism too. The Chinese look down on people with brown skin. Only farmers, who have to work in the sun, are dark.

Then there is the lack of understanding for culture and religion. The Cultural Revolution took care of that. None of this bodes well for the Tibetans: darker, poorer, with a deep attachment to their culture and faith. Put this together with the absolute power that was given to the local party officials in Tibet and the invasion of the country was a recipe for disaster.

But it wasn't easy to go and investigate all of this. For years it was impossible for a foreign correspondent living in Beijing to visit Tibet. This didn't change until the end of the 1990s. I applied immediately, in the month of May, but more important media people, like those working for CNN and the BBC, got to go first. Whenever I, as a representative of a Dutch newspaper, called the Ministry in Lhasa, the answer was that I was somewhere on the list and would receive a fax as soon as it was my turn. That fax never came. Somebody did tell me that I would probably get my turn in August. In August they said September. In October they declared that it was winter now, and much too cold, so there would be no more journalist visits for this year. I could try again in the spring. In the newspaper I read that there were special winter bargains to Tibet for tourists, so why was I kept out?

I complained at the Ministry in Beijing. A nice Chinese diplomat promised to help me. I renewed my application in February, but the answer stayed the same. That's when I decided that enough was enough, and changed my plans. I went to the Indian embassy to apply for a visa. Since I wanted to meet the refugees in Dharamsala in any case, but had planned to go to Tibet first, I could change things around. The Indians promised me a visa by that Friday. But when I came to pick it up, the Chinese man at the visa bureau declared that my case "had to be discussed first." That same day there was a phone call from Lhasa – asking if I could be in Tibet by Monday.

Even though I spent a year asking, and even if it did cost five hundred dollars a day, the officials of the Foreign Affairs Bureau in Lhasa did show me what I wanted to see. We spent the days meeting people. By six o'clock they would drop me off at the hotel and I would go into town by myself. I never had the feeling that I was followed.

Tibet was open once more. Diplomats, officials working for the United Nations, NGOs, foreign investors and of course tourists could all go in. Tourism was declared one of the pillars of the new economy. The authorities tried to increase the number of tourists fifty-fold in the coming years – in 2008 up to three million visitors were expected. The Olympic Games in Beijing brought another wave of media attention for Tibet. All over the West there were events, concerts, demonstrations, interviews with the Dalai Lama and even lip service by Western politicians. In Tibet itself, of course, there was a political crackdown, swiftly followed by a new campaign to lure back the tourists.

Over the years, the Tibet promoters have had lots of help from Hollywood. When two movies – *Seven Years in Tibet*, a Hollywood tale of an Austrian mountaineer who befriends the young Dalai Lama, and *Kundun*, the personal story of the Dalai Lama – came out, there was an upsurge in tourism to the region. Neither of these famous films were ever shown in Tibet. That, after all, that is China's policy: Tibet gets some of the profits, but freedom is out of the question.

I.

IS THE OLD ALWAYS BETTER?

R edi, vice-chairman of the Standing Committee of the National People's Congress, puts on his annual meet-the-press-face: small, round and annoyed. Exasperated, he stares at the rows of Western journalists in the Great Hall of the People in Beijing. He looks them straight in the eyes. After the third question about human rights issues in Tibet and the Dalai Lama, he bursts out, "All of you think that the old Tibet was so great. But we didn't have anything to eat. My brother died of starvation. Myself, I was bitten by dogs while I begged in the streets. I still have the scars. You call that a life?"

This tirade is followed by the annual gush of insults against the "Dalai Lama and his clique." The spiritual leader gets blamed for organizing just about every uprising since 1959. Whatever is wrong with Tibet, from economic hardship to political problems, it is all the Dalai Lama's fault. A journalist from the *Times* thinks that Redi is going too far. "How can you accuse the peace-loving Dalai Lama of all this? Don't you think you're losing the propaganda war?" he asks.

Redi becomes livid. "Since 1959, when their armed uprising failed, the Dalai Lama and his followers haven't given us a day of peace. They have constantly organized violent riots and even placed bombs. From the 1980s onwards, the Tibetan people could have lived quiet and prosperous lives. But the separatist activities never stopped. How can you call these people peaceful?"

Redi is not only annoyed with the Dalai Lama. He also hates Western journalists who keep on defending the Dalai Lama and who portray him, Redi, as a traitor.

"During these last years, the most ridiculous statements have been published in the Western press. You journalists live thousands of kilometers from my country, and you don't know anything about the old or the new Tibet. What do you want? To bring back the medieval reign of the Dalai Lama? You make up the most preposterous rumors. And you insult the Tibetan party leaders, but you don't know what you're talking about. You complain that there are new buildings in Tibet and that they don't look Tibetan. Well, new buildings look the same all over the world. Why do you think that the old is always better?"

Redi has it wrong. Nobody is saying that the old is always better. Even the exiled Tibetans in India know that the old social system in Tibet needed to be reformed. How that old system worked is an important dispute between the two sides. The Chinese talk about cruel landowners, monks and aristocrats, who kept and mistreated their slaves. According to Chinese statistics, 90 percent of Tibetans were slaves in the old society. They worked for free on the lands of the rulers. In exchange for their labor, they got to work on their own plot of land. Those who couldn't pay their taxes became house slaves at their masters' homes.

According to the *China Daily*, old Tibetan administration records of 1950, kept at the Archive of the Tibet Autonomous Region, show that 90 percent of Tibet's one million people were homeless. Of the 20,000 inhabitants of Lhasa at the time, more than 1,000 families lived as beggars.

Before 1959, the *China Daily* writes, Tibet was a society of "feudal serfdom under the despotic political-religious rule of lamas and nobles. The masses of serfs in Tibet did not even possess fundamental rights. Serf owners, principally local administrative officials, nobles, and upper-ranking lamas, owned all of Tibet's farmlands, pastures, forests, mountains and rivers as well as most of the livestock. The serfs lived no better than the slaves in the plantations in the southern states of America. The serf owners could sell or transfer their serfs, present them as gifts, or use them as mortgage payments for debts. They could even exchange them, molest them or maltreat them. When two serfs got married, the husband and wife still belonged to different owners and their children were fated to be serfs from the moment they were born."

This system was set in stone, the media state. "The statutory code of old Tibet stipulated that people were unequal in status by dividing people into three classes and nine ranks. In a peculiar law concerning the value of human life, it was written that the lives of people belonging to the highest rank of the upper class, such as a prince or leading Living Buddha, were calculated to be worth the weight of the dead body in gold, whilst the lives of people belonging to the lowest rank of the lower class, such as women, butchers, hunters and craftsmen, were worth a straw rope."

The judicial system of old Tibet gave monasteries and serf owners the right to judge, the media state, and punishment was cruel. "Punishments issued by the courts were extremely savage and cruel and included gouging out the eyes, cutting off the ears, hands or feet; pulling out tendons; throwing the criminal into water or shutting the criminal in a wooden case lined with nails facing inwards." (All quotes from *Chinatibetnews. com*, March 21, 2008).

The Chinese media also give plenty of personal evidence. "According to many original contracts preserved in the Archives of the Nationalities Cultural Palace and the Archive of the Tibet Autonomous Region, the manorial lords had the freedom to exchange serfs or present serfs to each other as gifts. Serfs had to pay high interest on their debts by doing corvée (unpaid labor) or by selling their own children. A certificate, written in the old form of the Tibetan language used before 1959 and kept as File no. MC 1015 at the Archives of the Nationalities Cultural Palace, reads: *Being unable to pay back the money and grain we owe Nedong Dekhang, we, Tsewang Rabten and my wife, serfs of the Dusong Manor, must give up our daughter Gensong Tonten and younger son Padma Tenzin to Dekhang to repay the debts. The descendants of their son and daughter will be Dekhang's serfs.*" (*China Daily*, April 10, 2008).

The Tibetan refugees in India have carried out their own studies of the old society in Tibet. In their publication *Truth From Facts* (one of Deng Xiaoping's favorite sayings) they state that Tibet's social system wasn't so bad, especially if you compare it to the situation in other Asian countries at that time. To start with, the most important leader, the Dalai Lama, was a reincarnation. That meant that he could be born into any kind of family, rich or poor. So leadership was not inherited, as it is in monarchies. Both the 13th and the 14th Dalai Lamas came from peasant families. Monks filled many of the lower government positions, and their nominations also had nothing do to with their backgrounds. Everybody, poor or rich, could enter a monastery and start a career.

The farmers – serfs, according to the Chinese – had legal status, the publication says. They possessed documents in which their rights were precisely stated. They could also go to court if they had a problem. There was no problem at all for a farmer to sue his master. The 13th Dalai Lama passed a law in 1909 that stipulated that all serfs who had a problem could come and complain directly to him. But, according to the Tibetans, such disputes didn't happen often, as the people treated each other decently due to their Buddhist principles. It was a religious duty for the rich to take care of the poor. Capital punishment didn't exist in the old Tibet and only the Supreme Court could hand out harsh punishments like dismembering hands. In 1898, Tibet enacted a law abolishing such forms of punishment, except in cases of high treason or conspiracy against the state.

According to the exiled Tibetans, monasteries were important institutions as they "performed religious functions for the state and served as schools, universities and centers for Tibetan art, craft, medicine and culture. The role of monasteries as highly disciplined centers of Tibetan education was the key to the traditional Tibetan way of life. Monasteries bore all expenses of their students and provided them with free board and lodging. Some monasteries had large estates; some had endowments, which they invested. But other monasteries had neither of these. They received personal gifts and donations from devotees and patrons. The revenue from these sources was often insufficient to provide the basic needs of large monk populations in some monasteries. To supplement their income, some monasteries engaged in trade and acted as moneylenders."

A small section of the Tibetan population, the publication says, mostly in U-Tsang province, were tenants. "They held their lands on the estates of aristocrats and monasteries, and paid rent to the estate-holders either in kind or they sent one member of the family to work as a domestic servant or an agricultural laborer. Some of these tenant farmers rose to the powerful position of estate secretary. (For this, they were labeled by the Chinese as "agents of feudal lords".) Other members of these families had complete freedom. They were entitled to engage in any business, follow any profession, join any monastery or work on their own lands. Although they were known as tenants, they could not be evicted from their lands at the whim of estate holders. Some of the tenants were quite wealthy."

The exiled Tibetans have their own personal stories, like that of Ms. Dhondup Chodon, who comes from a family that was of the poorest social strata in independent Tibet. Remembering her life before the Chinese occupation in her book *Life in the Red Flag People's Commune*, she says: "I belong to what the Chinese now term as serfs of Tibet. ... There were six of us in the family. ... My home was a two-storied building with a walled compound. On the ground floor we used to keep our animals. We had four yaks, 27 sheep and goats, two donkeys and a land-holding of four and a half *khel* (0.37 hectares). ... We never had any difficulty earning our livelihood. There was not a single beggar in our area."

In the end it is safe to assume that in the old Tibet there were good and bad masters, charitable and abusive monks. But, as the Tibetan exiles point out in their publication, whatever society existed in Tibet, it was not an excuse for China to invade the area. As they put it, "No country is allowed to invade, occupy, annex and colonize another country just because its social structure does not please it."

Real slaves and aristocrats from the old times are hard to find in Tibet nowadays, as these people are dying out. The stories they tell about their youths are not as bad as those that you read in the Chinese press. But at the same time their situation seemed worse than the portrayals of the exiled Tibetans.

In Lhasa I ask to interview a former aristocrat. The translator smiles kindly at me. "Aristocrats here don't like to talk about the past. I'm sure you can understand that?" What about a re-educated noble, one who is happy with the socialist state, I try again – but she just keeps shaking her head. In the end we find a former slave master totally by accident. It takes some careful coaxing before he agrees to talk about his youth.

This happens when we visit a school for orphans. A Tibetan orphan, who had been taken to India when she was small, founded it. Now she lives in Switzerland and there she does fund-raising to keep 30 kids in Lhasa in a house and in school. There are many street children in Tibet's capital, so those who get an education are lucky. The children in this house have an "acting father". He welcomes us into a small room, where the air is blue with burning incense.

The acting father used to be a teacher, he says. He worked at the local Tibetan school, earning a small salary but didn't build up a pension. So he is happy with his new job. At the orphanage he takes care of the children, sends them to school, helps them with their homework. I ask him about the Cultural Revolution, and find out that he spent those years in the countryside cutting wood because of his family background. The interview becomes difficult after this revelation, as there isn't much he wishes to say about the past.

His parents didn't seem to be oppressive torturers. "Long ago, in the old Tibet, society was different," the teacher says. "The rich always tried to give something to the poor. Tibetans are Buddhists and our religion stipulates that you have to help others. During the traditional festivals, like Tibetan New Year, the rich used to give money to the monasteries and the monks. We still do that, we give one yuan for each monk. The 15th of April is a day to give to beggars. But most well-to-do-families gave something to the poor three times a month. Often they gave food."

So did something change for the poor children, like the ones he takes care of here at the orphanage? The acting father thinks that in those times, just like now, it was all a question of luck. If you were lucky, a rich family or a master would take care of you.

"In my family we had an orphan. The parents of the girl had died and the child was deaf and mute. My parents gave her money. She couldn't go to school, of course, but she helped us with the housework. She is old now and still lives with us. In those villages that belonged to monasteries, the masters were responsible for the orphans. So it all depended on what kind of monks there were. Some would take care of the poor children and others wouldn't. Nobody would have set up an orphanage like this one. People in those times didn't understand that education was important."

After speaking to this man, I am lucky enough to interview a former slave. He does remember how the monks from the local monastery used to beat people, but there is no tirade against the separatists. Most of all, the former slave wishes a different existence for his children. With or without a plot of land to work on, life as a peasant is never easy.

BINTSI, THE FORMER SLAVE

"Our life has really improved. We used to know nothing. Nowadays, we are much better informed. We know about politics. The name of the Chinese prime minister? No idea. Yes, I have a TV, right over there. But I don't have time to watch it. Plus, I can't remember those Chinese names. But I know that the Chinese prime minister is a good leader. He's not too young and not too old."

Bintsi may not remember the names of the Chinese politicians, but he is aware that his fate is in their hands. "I hope the policy of the Party doesn't change any more," he says. The farmer now has his own plot of land, some cows and a spotless white house. Our guide from the Foreign Affairs Bureau has some trouble finding the place. We walk for half an hour over little mud paths that seem to lead nowhere before he finds the house. The door is locked. Bintsi brings the key with him. Inside, there are pictures of Chinese girls on the wall, one of them a smiling Air China stewardess. The toilet, a hole dug behind a low wall at the back of the house, is empty. Did the people here clean everything up because they were expecting a guest or is this not their house? I wonder. During the interview, an old woman shuffles in, says something to Bintsi and leaves again. Bintsi nods silently.

"Now I have 8.5 *mu* of land. My wife and I grow tsampa, wheat and potatoes. That way, I can take care of myself. We sell the yams and potatoes on the market. I earn about 4,500 yuan a year. I have my wife and two children. The kids attend secondary school, right here in the village. I hope they will work for the government when they grow up. They can become *Ganbu* (Chinese officials). Then they'll have an iron rice bowl and won't have to work as hard as we do. It's hard to be a farmer.

"I was born and raised here. We used to be part of the Sera monastery which is close by. This whole village belonged to them. My family worked on the land of the monks. Then we had our own parcels where we cultivated vegetables. There were different kinds of slaves. Some were called *Wula*, like we were, they had a low social standing and had to work for the monks the whole year round. Others had better positions and they only had to work during the harvest. The monastery had a special organization committee. The head of that group, a monk, was our master. We got a new master every three years.

"People hardly ever tried to run away. Where would you go? We had been living here for generations, so you didn't think about leaving. If you were caught running away, you could get beaten. There would be a kind of trial at the monastery and the monks would decide your punishment. Mostly you were beaten with a stick. Other slaves then had to carry out the punishment. When I was small, I never thought about running away. We had very little contact with people from other villages. The only way to escape being a slave was to become a monk.

"One day we heard that the Chinese army was on its way. People told terrible stories about them, how they killed everybody. But others said that if you went to work for the PLA, you would earn a good salary. In those times we were dependent on stories and rumors. We couldn't go and see for ourselves if we could work for the soldiers, the master wouldn't let us. We were also forbidden to say anything good about the approaching army.

"When they reached our village, we were scared to death. We all ran away into the mountains, where we camped for a week. The soldiers set up a meeting at the monastery. We sent a few delegates, whose task it was to see how dangerous the soldiers were. They came back and told us that the combatants were friendly, and didn't do anything bad. They had told them that we were liberated now. So slowly, one by one, we went back to our homes.

"Nothing much changed in the beginning. But a few years later, in 1959, the democratic reforms started. One day we heard that the masters had all been killed while trying to flee to India. The Chinese came back to our village and told us that they were going to divide the land among us. We had another meeting and they set up a People's Committee. We were still afraid. We didn't understand why those Chinese wanted to give us land. And there were rumors that the Dalai Lama would come back soon and that we would have to give the land back again.

"The cadres told us that the Dalai Lama had run away because there had been a riot in Lhasa and that he didn't want to adhere to the 17-point agreement. We had no idea which agreement they were talking about. The Dalai Lama was our god, and we worshiped him. So those cadres tried to tell us that our god had done something wrong. We were worried something bad would happen to us, because the gods weren't respected any more and people said bad things about them. I thought that maybe the advisors and ministers of the Dalai Lama had done bad things. The Dalai Lama himself was very young, and didn't really have anything to say. He couldn't even decide what he wanted to eat. When he left for India, we were convinced that someone had kidnapped him.

"But the cadres told us that in front of the Potala Palace, there was a huge prison. The Dalai Lama was supposed to be the Buddha of compassion, they said, but he lived right next to an overcrowded jail. Because of their arguments, we slowly changed our ideas. We still believe in Buddhism, that's our tradition. But now we believe in the right way, we don't just follow blindly. I still think that the basic theory of Buddhism is good.

"Then the Cultural Revolution started, and I was made a Red Guard. I had the right family background for that. They told us that we had to fight against devils and evils. In the beginning, we still received orders about who or what to attack, but soon things got out of hand. In the end, we just destroyed everything that was old: yak butter lamps, for instance, and all old Tibetan things we could find. It was a very strong campaign. When I look back now, I think we were crazy in those times. We just bothered everybody without knowing why. We didn't know any political theories; I had never been to school. This whole revolution was an enormous waste of time and energy. Luckily, the elders still worked the land, so we did have food. Not a lot, but enough to get by. At that time, the land didn't belong to us any more either. We had become a commune and were supposed to do everything together, so people didn't work very hard.

"In 1978 the head of our village committee told us that it was time for a new structure, the Household Responsibility System. So we got some land for ourselves again. With that, one of the hardest parts of my life was over. The hardest parts were before Liberation, when I was young, and during the Cultural Revolution.

"Nowadays I'm not scared any more that the Dalai Lama will come back and take away our land. Even if he comes back, the Communist Party will protect me. The party is very powerful. But the Dalai Lama is also our spiritual leader, so I would like to see him come back. Maybe we could have the same system here as they have in Hong Kong: one country, two systems. I do hope that the party policy stays the way it is now. We get money now if we work hard. During the Cultural Revolution, when there were communes, it wasn't like that.

"The monastery is open again, but I don't know the monks there any more. Even when I was small, we would only be in contact with the monk who was our master, and he ran away to India. The new monks are all young. There are just a few old ones, but I don't know them. I have heard that there are two kinds of monks nowadays: those who want to be like playboys, they trade, earn money and even get married. But there are also real religious people, who spend their lives studying Buddhism. I respect that last group. Nowadays, there is good organization in the monasteries. A Democratic Management Committee governs them. I never go there, but I heard that it's much better than in the old times."

2.

A COUNTRY OF BEGGARS

One day, I found Ngawang's wife and two of their youngest children begging on the street in Lhasa. Nothing special about that, it's full of beggars here and normally speaking I don't even notice them any more. But the youngest child looked so pitiful and endearing, I should never have looked in his eyes. Pieter and I loaded the whole sticky bunch in the car and took them home. Tsitoka and Doma spent hours scrubbing the bathtub after the whole family had taken a bath. The mother told us that Sanchoe, the smallest, was in fact the oldest. Samchoe was supposed to be three years old: his fontanel is still open, he can't walk, can't talk, et cetera. So we concluded that mother is slightly delusional. We took all of them to the hospital for a check-up. And then? I already started to regret my not-so-clever good deed when an opportunity presented itself.

The authorities got this absurd idea to build a four-lane highway in front of the Tashi Lopur monastery in Shigatse (average of three cars an hour) and the wall around our compound there had to be moved a few meters inwards. So they broke down the old wall and promised to build it up again within a few days. Those few days have become two months by now and there is no end in sight, not even with those thick glasses we distribute here for the nearly blind. The problem was that our house/office was now visible from the road and the extremely curious Tibetans saw their chance and started sightseeing on the compound. Apparently we got some good publicity because the amount of visitors grew dramatically. At the strangest moments I would find a beautifully dressed-up Tibetan pushing his nose flat against our windows.

So we created a perfect job for Ngawang, the father. He is now our guard in Shigatse and the amusement park is closed from now on. Ngawang and Genzien (with child again; Ngawang doesn't seem to be capable of much, but he does know how to make babies) live happily ever after in the little house of the Red Cross. As a sign of respect, people here stick out their tongues, so Ngawang spends his days with his tongue on the floor. If you even point at me, you will have a big problem with Ngawang. So I managed to solve several problems in one day: Ngawang gets a salary and lives for free, while the rest of the staff here tries to convince his wife that babies really should eat more than just tsampa (flattened flour). It's beautiful to see. Samchoe is still, like all the other children, a very quiet child. Wherever you put him, he stays. He doesn't crawl away, or cry, or anything. If you're not careful, you could just forget he's there. We try our best to get some fruits and vegetables into the child, to give him some energy. Finally, we see something happen. Amazing! His eyes have started to move.

(From the newsletter of Tineke Ceelen, Red Cross, Lhasa)

"We have become a country of beggars", a Tibetan traveler once concluded after a visit to Tibet. The Chinese government may state that the poor are better off nowadays than in the old Tibet, but the reality is that progress has been minimal. The poor cultivate their land but, just like many Chinese, they have the feeling that they have lost a lot of valuable time to political campaigns. As one Tibetan in exile said, "Fifty years is a long time. Who says we couldn't have developed without the Chinese? In fact, it's their political campaigns that kept us from economic progress."

The Tibetan cadres often try to convince the outside world that the region is undergoing rapid growth. Delivering statistics that prove how China is assisting in this process is part of Redi's yearly press conference. "Before the democratic reforms in 1959, Tibet was behind in both social and economic development, as it had been oppressed by despotic lamas and aristocrats. After the peaceful liberation, and especially since the open door policy and economic reforms, the state took special measures and gave enough material, financial and human support for the region to move forwards," he reads from a piece of paper. We journalists all get a copy to take home.

When you read the Chinese media, you would think that Tibet is on its way to becoming an economic tiger. "Tibet's gross domestic product (GDP) is expected to grow 10.1 percent year-on-year to reach 39.2 billion yuan (5.8 billion US dollars) this year, a senior local official has said. It would be the 16th year that the Tibetan Autonomous Region in southwest China has had double-digit economic growth, said Qiangba Puncog, chairman of the regional government. The fixed assets investment would hit 31 billion yuan, up 14.3 percent from a year earlier, he told an economic work conference held Sunday. "Farmers and herdspeople are the beneficiaries of the economic development," he said, citing that per capita net income for them would reach 3,170 yuan, up 13.7 percent year-on-year." (Xinhua news agency, December 22, 2008).

Of course there has been some progress in Tibet. In the eighties and nineties, there were many success stories. At that time, investors from Lhasa were able to trade stocks and bonds for the first time. The first investment company opened its doors and a Tibetan hotel group went public on the Shanghai stock exchange. It worked. During a pre-sale in Lhasa, investors fought over the shares. The airplanes to Tibet were filled with brokers carrying suitcases of cash and oxygen masks. All this enthusiasm, however, had nothing to do with the economic situation, and everything to do with politics. "This is the first stock that has been issued by a national minority corporation. The authorities will never let this company go under, whatever happens," one investor declared. He was right. As soon as the one-yuan stock appeared on the Shanghai exchange, it went up to 3.5 and ended at 6.2 that same day. Within a short time, there were 1,800 stockholders in Tibet, the *China Daily* reported.

And some party leaders honestly tried to improve the situation. Hu Yaobang, after seeing the communes in Tibet, immediately met with the leaders of the Tibetan Autonomous Region and asked them if they had thrown all the money that Beijing had sent to Tibet into the Yarlung River. He demanded that in three years' time, the Tibetan standard of living should be brought back to the level of 1959. With that declaration, he nullified all Chinese propaganda about progress due to the Chinese liberation. Hu also promised to send 85 percent of the Chinese cadres home. But the party leader didn't stay in power long enough to carry out his threats. After he was removed from his position, the local authorities in Lhasa could do as they pleased again. On paper, the production figures were rising, while the poor kept begging on the streets.

Whenever the Chinese authorities admit that the economy in Tibet is in a sorry state, they blame the Tibetans. Their "separatist demonstrations" for independence are bad for economic stability and scare investors away, they say.

"Qiangba Puncog said economic growth was achieved against the backdrop of a string of difficulties this year, including the March 14 riot, an earthquake in Damxung County, the snow disaster in Shannan Prefecture and the global financial crisis. To cope with the challenges, the local government published a series of regulatory measures to keep the economy growing steadily and rapidly, he said. In addition, the central government invested more than 16 billion yuan in Tibet this year to support development. But the tourism industry would shrink this year because of the March 14 riot that led to a temporary suspension of tour groups. The tourist arrivals would reach 2.2 million this year, Qiangba Puncog said. He did not provide an estimate about the tourism revenue. The riot caused a 69 percent year-on-year decline in first-half tourist arrivals in this plateau region, to just 342,000 people, the Tibetan Autonomous Regional Tourism Bureau said." (Xinhua, December 22, 2008).

The exiled Tibetans in India advise keeping two things in mind when reading Chinese statistics about economic growth. First of all, they say, Chinese figures are not published to give readers statistical insight, but are created to prove the success of a political policy. And second, it's not the Tibetans, but the Chinese who profit most from economic development and subsidies in the region.

The exiles in India accuse China of colonial exploitation. "The emphasis was placed on Tibet's integration with China rather than on local self-sufficiency. Tibet was providing China's rich coastal region with energy, minerals and timber. In return, Tibet was receiving Chinese "skilled" settlers who brought "technical, managerial and business skills" to the region and helped open Tibet's market for Chinese manufactured goods. This massive influx of Chinese settlers further marginalized the Tibetan people, economically and socially," they claim in *Truth from Facts*, an information brochure from the Tibetan government in exile.

The exiles have their own figures. "In 1984 the Chinese government initiated 43 development projects, following up with 62 additional projects in 1994. These projects aimed to "develop the Tibetan economy and society" in Central Tibet. However, these initiatives did not result in the development of any significant Tibetan-run projects. Instead they have mainly benefited Chinese urban dwellers and strengthened China's control over Tibet. For example, the projects initiated in 1984 alone brought 60,000 Chinese into Tibet, causing 30,000 Tibetans from 18 work units to lose their jobs. Rural areas in Tibet still have no access to electricity, education, healthcare and safe drinking water facilities."

Through the years, economic growth in Tibet was much slower than in other Chinese provinces. Tibet remained one of the poorest regions in the country. According to statistics of the exiles, Tibet's economy can be compared to the poorest in Africa. "With an estimated per capita income of $80 in 1990, an adult literacy rate of 21.7 per cent and an average life expectancy of 40 years, the "TAR" scores just 0.087 on the UNDP's Human Development Index for 1991. This would theoretically place it between Chad and Djibouti at position 153 out of the world's 160 nations."

Because of the Chinese influence, it has proven very difficult for foreigners to give development aid to Tibet. One year, the European Union wanted to invest nine billion dollars in agricultural projects for Tibetans. It was supposed to become the biggest foreign investment project ever in Tibet. But then the *Observer* newspaper discovered that right after the project's approval, thousands of houses were constructed for a huge group of Chinese laborers. They were getting the jobs, not the Tibetans. Similarly, the second phase of an irrigation program of the United Nations was postponed when the foreigners discovered that Chinese workers were constructing everything.

The Panchen Lama in his speeches complained bitterly about the economic policy towards Tibet. "In the State Planning Commission's report, there were many proposals for poverty alleviation in many areas. But these proposals did not say a word on the minority regions. Raising this point in the Standing Committee meeting, I said, "There is nothing wrong in you becoming prosperous first. We will wear threadbare garments and beg for food. But does that do you proud?" These claims, which were delivered to the National People's Congress in Beijing, are not far from those of the exiled Tibetans now. "During my visit to Kham last year I noticed a great deal of devastation caused by large-scale and indiscriminate deforestation. I saw huge landslides caused by this. Industries with the potential to generate high revenue are closed down in minority regions. To take an example, there was a cigarette factory in Taklo-Tron, Yunnan, which could be very profitable. But this factory had to be closed down because of a shortage of trained manpower and the poor quality cigarettes it produced. This despite the fact that it was using high quality raw materials. The industries in Shanghai, on the other hand, do not use high quality raw materials, but they have trained personnel and the best possible technology, resulting in high quality goods and profit."

The Tibetan cadres who are educated by the Chinese believe that economic progress will soon come to the region. People like Redi and Tari, the woman who tells her story next, know how far they have come. One was a beggar, the other a shepherd, and both are now in government positions. So they believe that this road is open for every Tibetan. Although these former beggars don't really believe in communism, those that I met in Beijing and Lhasa end up living a better life. Redi always plays his role with such vehemence that you really get the feeling he believes what he says, even when he reads senseless statistics about his home region. The man with the small round face gets really offended when someone suggests that he is betraying his country. "We are the nationalists," he says. "Over there, in India, that's where the traitors are."

Tari is a lot less dramatic. But she does show me, while telling her story, that she is now in a position to start all kinds of projects to help the Tibetans. And that is more than the exiles in India are able to do.

TARI CIRENYUZHEN, THE TIBETAN CADRE

Cirenyuzhen is the Chinese translation of her name. It's how she introduces herself. Tari is a tough woman in traditional clothing. She smokes cigarettes and complains about her eyesight, which deteriorated when she worked with nomads. Nowadays, Tari works for the Tibetan

Art Association. She publishes a magazine about Tibetan culture, so that the Chinese can learn from it. And she tries to conserve art. Behind the building where she works, there is a workshop. A living Buddha teaches poor youths sculpting according to old techniques. The colorful masks and statues of Buddhas and yaks are made with pieces of cloth that are soaked in a natural kind of plaster. This way, the young apprentices learn a skill which will help them earn a living, and the old ways of making models will be preserved. As well as a writer, Tari is a great storyteller. Anecdotes from her life keep us listening for almost four hours.

"When I was small, I herded sheep. My parents were farmers in Chamdo. They owned plots of land and they had some animals. From the time I was six, I looked after the cattle. When you were eight, the age that you changed teeth, you were allowed to go into the mountains with the yaks. The adults always joked about that; as soon as you showed holes in your mouth, you were old enough to go far.

"We lived with eight families in a village. A few boys were sent to the monastery close by. That was the tradition in that time. My father loved culture and he taught us girls to read and write too. We only read religious texts. We learned those by heart, without really knowing what they meant. I was happiest when people visited our village and told stories. In those stories, the animals and the sun could talk. My big dream for the future in that time was to become the main character in one of those stories.

"But later, the visitors started to tell scary tales. They talked about the approaching People's Liberation Army. We were afraid of soldiers, as we had dealt with the Tibetan warriors who were fighting the Chinese, and they were no good. Once, those Tibetan army officers sent us a message. They wanted all the women of the village to come feed their horses. We knew what they were planning to do. Why would these soldiers only want women? When they came, we all ran away. We went to hide in the house of a rich landowner, because the soldiers wouldn't dare to go there.

But they did take two of our horses. My father went after them, to beg them to return the animals, and in the end they gave him one. This is why we hated the Tibetan warriors.

"The first Chinese soldiers made a very different impression. We were terrified of them too. When they arrived, my mother was so scared she didn't know what to do, and in the end she decided to be as friendly as possible. She took a Tibetan prayer shawl, ran outside, and hung it around the neck of the leader. We were all hiding in the house and were watching through small cracks in the wall. We were surprised when the army leader took out a better shawl and hung it around my mother's neck. A translator told us that the soldiers didn't want to hurt us, they were here to help. If we gave them food, they would pay us.

"Some time later something else happened to me that impressed me even more. Two soldiers came by one day, and they lost a bag. I was sitting in the field, together with another girl, looking after the animals. I think she still lives in that place. We saw the bag fall and the girl sent me to get it. It was filled with all kinds of things we liked: books, money and things we had never seen before, like a torch. We threw away the books, my friend took the money and I got the torch. That night, the Chinese soldiers came back. They held a meeting and explained that they had lost something. They said that the money and the things weren't that important, but they really wanted their books back. I kept my mouth shut, of course. I had hidden the torch in the fold of my dress. Then, when we arrived home, my brother pulled at my dress and the lamp fell out. My father took me to see the soldiers; I showed them the place where we had dumped the books. Instead of punishment, the soldiers gave my father 20 yuan, a small fortune for us. That's how I started to trust them. So when I got the chance to work for them, I didn't hesitate.

"By that time, I remember, more and more visitors came to our village. Every time someone came, a villager would go with him; I remember how strange that was. One day a man arrived and he said that he needed four people to go help the Chinese army. All the names of the adults were written on pieces of paper and put in a pot. That day, we were unlucky. Three people in my family were chosen; my mother and my two brothers all had to go. There was nothing we could do. We were simple people. I was just a dumb peasant girl, so we did what we were told.

"My family was put to work close to Lhasa. My brothers heard that they could study in Shenyang, in the north of China. So they left to get an education, like hundreds of others. My mother stayed in Lhasa to wait for them. That went on for three years. I was 15 years old by that time, and wanted to see my mother. One family member promised to take me to Lhasa. We left with a whole caravan of camels and horses loaded with goods and food. But after one day, bandits robbed us. My uncle decided to go back to the village, but I wasn't turning around.

"So, my friend and I ran away. We took as much food as we could carry. There were no roads, only paths where people had walked for hundreds of years. At night we took shelter with families. Our luggage turned out to be much too heavy, so we started to leave things everywhere. We gave it to the people who housed us, or we just left it by the side of the road. That way we walked for 20 days. When we arrived in Lhasa, I was amazed. I had never seen so many houses and so many people in one place. We asked everybody on the street if they knew my mother, and in the end we found our former neighbor who took us to my mother. In fact, Lhasa wasn't that big in those times. It was just one main road. My mother gave me a long speech, because I shouldn't have run away the way I had, but I didn't care. I was happy to see her again.

"In Lhasa I went to work for the PLA. It was a very simple job. We didn't have to do anything, just watch movies. That's when I discovered that the world was big and that there were other countries. We watched many war movies. I can still remember one story about a very brave boy who was captured by Japanese soldiers. He was very clever and managed to escape. I don't remember what happened after that, just being impressed.

Of course we didn't understand a word of what they were saying, as these films were all in Chinese. But I thought they were amazing. We also had a translator who taught us Chinese, and after that, they taught us ideology.

"In 1963 I was sent to Beijing. We went with 13 students: 12 girls and one boy. We had a great time, you can imagine. The boy had a small barrel of yak butter with him and he refused to share any of it. After a few days in a boiling hot train, it started to stink mightily. Beijing was very clean. In those days, the Chinese worked very hard and kept everything spotless. They asked us why we smelled so bad. So our friend ended up throwing his yak butter in the toilet. We laughed ourselves silly.

"When I got back to Tibet, the Cultural Revolution had started. There were wall posters everywhere. I got a job as the head of a village in Amdo province. I stayed there for 33 years and eventually became head of the province.

"The atmosphere during the Cultural Revolution was very threatening. I was 23 years old, I felt tough and I carried a gun with me. I was ready to die, and I was convinced that was not going to take long. One day, Red Guards came and said they wanted to topple me. I showed them a document with the stamps of the government and told them, "You show me the same document, with the same stamps that says that I am fired, and I'll go." So they left.

"Another day Red Guards came to demolish the temple. I said, "Are you sure you want to do that?" They started insulting me and accusing me of being a Buddhist. So I said, "The people built this temple, so I suppose it's fine if the people break it as well." I went to sit in my office until they were done. Now that I work for the Cultural Association, those same people come to ask me for money to restore the temple. That's when I get really mad. Nevertheless, we did manage to rebuild many of them. There are a few we left, as we don't invest in places where the monks behave badly.

"In our area there were 126 monasteries, and after the Cultural Revolution they were all gone. Except for one. A very clever man managed that building. When the Red Guards came, he went to hide behind the Buddha statue. When the revolutionaries started to pull at it, he shouted, "Don't touch me!" The Guards, all of them Tibetans, got the shock of their lives. They were revolutionaries, but deep down they were still superstitious, so they ran off. I shook with laughter when I heard that story.

"Amdo is a disastrous place. Nobody wanted to work there, but I saw a chance to do something useful for the people. In winter there is so much snow that the nomads' yaks start to starve. That's when I would start calling everybody to ask for money, so we could buy new animals for the people. Every family would then get a few new yaks. Sometimes you hoped that a family's animals would all die, because then they would get new ones from us. Better to get new ones than to be stuck with a few starved, weak, old ones.

"Disasters kept repeating themselves in Amdo. We had one in 1985, another one in 1989 and a year later there was another. The yaks keep dying and people have a hard life. But we never heard that anyone died of hunger or cold. That's already a great achievement for the local authorities. We *ganbus* worked hard to keep the people alive. But something structural has to happen, and that costs a lot of money. The quality of the grasslands has to improve and those nomads have to learn to live in houses. In our neighborhood, 80 percent already have a more permanent dwelling.

"In the province I also met my husband. He was the village doctor, but then changed job and became a *ganbu* too. After 33 years, I became too old to work in such disaster-prone territory. During the last blizzard I almost became snow-blind. Look at my eyes, one is almost blind. That's why I asked for a transfer to the big city. It's also better for the children. One of my daughters works for the TV station here, she has a program in Tibetan. The other manages the post office.

"Here, I can do what I love, which is to preserve Tibet's culture and traditions. It wasn't easy to set up the workshop. I spent a long time looking for a teacher who knew how to make these statues. I went to all the monasteries in the area. The living Buddha here had to come out of the monastery to do this work. He already educated one group of young people, and they have their own workshops now. Once he becomes too old to teach, we will have a problem. I wouldn't know where to find another teacher who knows these techniques. And it's important. So many skills got lost during the Cultural Revolution. Things we did hundreds of years ago are unknown now. We have to try to save as much as we can."

ZHAXI, IMITATOR OF MAO ZEDONG

"I don't see why we would not be allowed to be friends with a foreigner," Song Que says. "Yes, and besides, you have to help him," Zhaxi tells me. We're eating in a fancy Chinese restaurant in Beijing. Zhaxi insists on paying the bill. He doesn't need my help. As one of the few actors allowed to imitate Mao Zedong, he's got a good job. Song Que's position is not that great. He works as a teacher at the Huangsi temple in Beijing.

I meet my two new friends after my visit to the temple. I thought that the research institute would be a good place to start looking for Tibetans living in Beijing, but of course this turns out to be an impossible idea. An old Chinese *shifu*, or custodian, greets me, and informs me that it is his job to keep unwanted visitors out. A foreign journalist who thinks she can just walk into the temple makes him visibly nervous. He takes me into his dark little room next to the entrance and shows me a piece of paper that is lying on his desk. It's a list of the kinds of people he is to deny entry. Foreigners are at the top.

That's not so strange, as the China-Tibet Buddhist Institute is located inside the temple. A few hundred Lamas get lessons in their own culture and Buddhism, and of course in political doctrine like the ideas of Deng

Xiaoping. It's a hotspot for problems. The combination of Tibetan Lamas and imposed political classes always leads to trouble.

While I'm standing there, reading through the list the old man is showing me, a young Tibetan intellectual approaches. "You tell her," the old man asks him desperately. The young man, Song Que, explains again that foreigners are not permitted here. "But," he says brightly, "you are welcome to come to my house. I'll show you my life's work."

In his apartment, Song presents hundreds of sheets of rice paper with Chinese and Tibetan characters. Just looking at them makes me dizzy. Song explains that it's an English-Chinese-Tibetan dictionary and he's been working on it for six years.

Song's problem is finding a publisher. "Maybe you can help me with that? In China there are a few publishers who can print Tibetan. I called them, but they said I would have to pay for it myself." I write an article about Song for a Dutch magazine, showing the intellectual's picture. A few months later Song tells me: "When the authorities saw that I was a known writer abroad, they gave me the money to publish the book."

Song, his family and his friends all come from what is now the province of Qinghai. As the region isn't at such a high altitude as Lhasa, the Tibetans from this place can live in Beijing without getting sick. But they don't become Chinese. They speak Mandarin with strong Tibetan accents and, as soon as they are alone, speak only Tibetan.

In the end it's Zhaxi who agrees to tell his life story. Zhaxi always comes whenever Song Que visits. He is a confident man and he's rich. He drives around in a new Volkswagen Santana and he spends a lot of time talking on his fancy cellular phone. Every weekend Zhaxi is fully booked, so he always visits me during the week. Besides being lucrative, it's also an honor to imitate Mao Zedong. You need special permission because the authorities want to make sure only good quality Maos appear on TV. The Tibetan plays his role perfectly. When he isn't acting, he's a lively man who likes to tell tall tales. But once he's dressed as Mao, he changes his way of walking, starts to stare ahead and speaks with a low voice. Most of the time he keeps a stern silence. "When you're dressed as Mao, you have to be careful what you say," he explains.

But even the rich and confident Zhaxi can be intimidated. We find that out on the day we want to take a picture of him on Tiananmen Square, under the giant portrait of the real Mao. The photographer has a car with diplomatic license plates, so he figures he can do what he wants, including parking right under the portrait. Immediately Chinese policemen come swarming from all directions. The situation instantly turns Zhaxi and Song into nervous wrecks, even though the police don't say or do anything. "Hurry up. Are you still not done?" Zhaxi asks the photographer with a tortured look. Song has walked away from us and is looking on from a safe distance.

The fact that Zhaxi makes a living imitating the leader who invaded his country, and whose political campaigns got innumerable Tibetans killed, doesn't pose a problem for him. "I'm an actor and this is a part," he shrugs.

"I'm an artist and in a poor place like Qinghai there are very few cultural events. So I came to Beijing.

"I was born in Qinghai, Guoluo, in the Tibetan region. When I was one year old, my mother gave me to another family. My father died in 1958, during the liberation by the People's Army. No, he didn't fight or anything, he was at home. My mother was seven months pregnant when he passed away. Why she gave me away, I still don't know. I did ask her once and she answered, "Because that other family didn't have any children and they really wanted you." But that's hard to imagine. A child is not an object you can give away as a present. My foster parents told me the opposite. They said that they didn't really want me, but that my mother insisted on giving me to them. So I guess I'll never know what was really behind it all.

"In any case, my new family took good care of me. I went to elementary and secondary school in the city. My new father was a driver and he often took me along if he had to drive somewhere. Life was good, until my foster mother got pregnant after all. She had two sons over the next two years. That's when they didn't want me any more. I was around 15 years old then. The relationship with the family went downhill fast and so one day my father took me to Hainan, another district. I lived there for one year, until I passed the entry exam to the university in Xi'an.

"I had always loved art, dancing, singing. At school I was one of the best students. My parents didn't like it that I sang so much. They didn't understand art at all and didn't know it could become a profession. They wanted me to study and then become a *ganbu*. But at school I had a teacher who did recognize my talents. He decided that I needed to study music, so my parents didn't argue.

"Until I went to Xi'an, I had only been in Tibetan regions. In Xi'an it was the first time that I had to live with the Han Chinese. I really had to get used to them. The food was different, but the hardest thing was their mentality. The Han Chinese are not truthful. They always say nice things and agree with everything. They'll tell you, "Sure, I'll help you," but they won't do anything for you. They'll tell you that they tried, but it didn't work. Then they'll disappear for half a year and come back with new promises.

"After my study, I was put to work with the Qinghai theater group. I sang there for two years. One day, a stranger approached me after the performance. He told me that he was one of my relatives and that my real mother wanted to see me. I was 22 years old. I went with him and that's when I met my mother for the first time. She had heard that there had been a problem between me and my foster parents and felt guilty. So she wanted to make sure I was alright. She is a nomad and she leads a normal existence. She's got some sheep and yaks, so I don't send her any money. I used to send money to my stepmother, as both of her sons are jobless.

They had to live in the old house and only got 300 yuan unemployment benefits. When she died, I went and paid for the funeral. I wanted to leave all the bad feelings behind. After all, she looked after me for 15 years and that's more than my own mother did. So I still think about her with kindness.

"I changed jobs after a few years. They put me to work as a teacher at the conservatory in Qinghai. I didn't really want that, but the authorities decided it for me. I taught for eight years. It wasn't really my cup of tea, I prefer acting. So in 1992, I decided to leave for Beijing. The director of the school at first didn't want to let me go. He refused to arrange a scholarship for me, but I decided I could pay my own way. At that time, it wasn't so expensive to study and I had some savings. I knew that the cultural level in Beijing was much higher than in the provinces, so I applied to study here. I lived off 250 yuan a month. In the canteen, I always chose the cheapest food, the dish without meat.

"Then one day my friend saw an advertisement on TV about the National Acting Competition. He told me, "Zhaxi, you should apply." My friends already knew that I could imitate Mao Zedong. I look like him, and I know how to imitate accents. Whenever we were hanging out together, my friends always insisted that I play Mao, and also prime minister Zhou Enlai. At first I was hesitant about the competition. "Those people are professional actors, and I'm just an amateur," I said. But my friend told me that I should at least try. So I went.

"I was surprised to get through the first selection rounds. We started off with a few thousand candidates. There were different categories; I was in the one for historical figures. The farther I got, the more seriously I started to prepare for my role. During the finals, there were only 20 of us. I was still completely flabbergasted that I had gotten that far. And then I won.

"When you win a national competition like that, you don't get prize money or a contract. But you do become famous. All the newspapers wrote about me. I thought I was at the start of a long and successful career. What could go wrong now?

"But that turned out to be disappointing. It is now many years ago that I won the competition and until now, I still haven't played in any movies. I act in TV series and go to cultural events, but I was never on the big screen. You need good connections to get there and I don't have those. All those Han with their big stories always promise me a part in a movie, or to introduce me to a famous director. It has cost me tens of thousands of yuan in wining and dining expenses; some I have taken out for dinner at least ten times, without any result.

"The Dalai Lama? Yes, my parents used to tell me about him. I knew that he was an important Buddha and lived in India. I didn't know why, exactly. My father used to say that there were many Tibetans in India and that was why he lived there. Later, when I became older, I heard on the news that there was a problem. Yes, of course it would be good if there were a solution. Can we change the subject?

"The problem with Han Chinese is that they are not religious. Being a Buddhist for us means that you don't live for yourself, you also help others. It's like that in the village. If the neighbors see that someone isn't home, they go to check that he didn't forget to lock the door. But the Han only think about money. I have one friend who is a Han. He plays Zhou Enlai. Whenever I am asked for a performance, and the director wants to know if I know others, I always introduce him. But would he do that for me? Not at all. If someone asks him whether he knows other actors, he says, "No, I don't know anybody." Or "I can't reach anyone else. I'm the only one who's available."

"It's also difficult to get a job when you're from an ethnic minority. Whenever I apply for a job, they read my name on my identity card and they immediately see that I'm Tibetan. And then they start to ask questions: "Does he speak Mandarin?" I always answer, "Watch my performance, and judge then." After they've seen me act, they get embarrassed and say, "Good, very good."

"Sometimes I think I came into this business too late. The actor who is the best Mao imitator started ten years before me. I don't want to boast, but when I look at his acting, there's nothing I couldn't do. I would love to play in a foreign movie. Maybe you can help me with that. Whenever you hear that foreigners are going to make a movie with Mao Zedong in it, you could introduce me.

"I will do this job as long as I can. Nowadays, I also audition for other roles. And I do some trading on the side. I can live from my performances. I earn 10,000 yuan for each performance, but it's so unreliable. Actors used to be employed by the state and they used to earn a stable, meager salary. Nowadays, the TV stations are privatized. Investors look for a group of actors and a director and they make their own programs and movies. Then they sell the production to TV stations. Because of this, there are fewer movies about Mao. Those rich people invest in soap operas. I do have work enough, though. Apart from TV, there are also the shops and companies. People like to have a Mao imitator perform during the opening of their enterprise. It's easy work too. I just need to walk around a bit.

"Besides acting, I also want to get married. That is not as easy as it sounds. I did have a girlfriend, but she was a Han and I want to marry a Tibetan. But there aren't enough Tibetan women here. Those who live in Qinghai don't want to come to Beijing. They know what life is like over here. The nomads on the grasslands don't know about life, but women who work for companies travel often. They come to Beijing for meetings or just for fun. And then they immediately conclude that they don't want to live here.

"One of them told me: "In Beijing you can't even ask directions. People ignore you if they don't know you. In our village, if a visitor arrives, we give him food and shelter and walk with him to his destination. But in Beijing, people don't trust anybody." And maybe they are right. There are a lot of evil people here in the big city. But I do want to stay here. For an artist like me, this is where the opportunities are."

3.

ABANDONED IN THE SNOW

After two hours of sliding and slipping on ice, I had to vomit. This time not from travel sickness or food poisoning, but from the scene before me. There were kilometers of cadavers. There must have been thousands. Snow, ice and dead yaks was all we saw. We talked with 20 nomad families. They had lost virtually all their cattle. Of the 300 yaks, only eight were still alive; two of the 300 sheep had survived; 20 goats of what used to be 150. And so on and so forth. The nomads were desperate. One man, who had only 12 sheep left, begged us on his knees to take him and his surviving animals to a warmer place. Without these last sheep, there would be no way to reproduce and he would have no more livelihood, like hundreds of others in his situation. Another man, who walked around in soaking wet cloth sneakers, asked for food. He had given everything to his animals. To no avail, apparently, as the area around his tent was covered with carcasses.

And the cold, God, the cold. In Nyerond my toothpaste was frozen. Here, far after Neyerong, I hardly dare to get out of the car. Ten minutes outside and my eyelashes are frozen, my hands and feet so cold that I could scream from pain. The nomads live in this weather, in tents. It makes me furious, the way the world ignores this disaster. A truck with nomads has arrived in our Tingri settlement. They are cold and position themselves around a bonfire to get a little warmth.

Standing on the back of a truck in minus 20 degrees Celsius, I can imagine they're freezing.

After four more hours of sliding and careful maneuvering, we reach Nijalam. Why do people live here? It's literally in the middle of nowhere, stuck between two Himalayan mountains. The place has become busy now. Trucks full of nomads block the road. It's actually a colorful sight. The snow has been shoved aside and has frozen again, forming big piles of ice by the side of the road. The heaps reach my waist. Life must be unbearably hard here. And the dirt! Everywhere there is people's excrement, urine, toilet paper, food scraps and God knows what else. You can't imagine the filth. The public toilet makes me retch. No wonder there are epidemics. What are we doing here?

But one hour in Nijalam does give us a lot of information. All of a sudden I start to see things clearly. Tibet is the last place on earth without international aid. In Africa they at least had the missionaries. But here there is nothing except for the local authorities. I feel sorry for the doctor at the local hospital who has to answer our questions. Poor man, what does he know? He only knows that he lacks medicine to treat these snow-blind people. He has to treat frozen hands and feet but can't do anything without medicine. He never heard of prevention. The snow came a few weeks earlier than expected. So it's logical that the animals froze to death and there was not enough wood to keep the people warm. Except for this local hospital, there is no help whatsoever. And this one hospice is in a sad state. A patient is rotting away in his own filth. Used needles are put aside on a tray, waiting for the next victim.

I feel helpless and angry. Not because of the local population, but with the world of NGOs and aid organizations. "There is no structure there, so we can't do anything. We only work with local organizations and Tibet is not a major-priority country," one of them told me. "And anyway, it's not as bad as in Africa. They're not dying

by the dozens. They are used to it here. Survival of the fittest." She is
right, of course, that's the way it works. Where there is help, more aid
will be given. You can earn money in places where you can film the
dying. Nobody gives a dime for frozen limbs.

Red Cross posters are hanging on the wall of the hospital. The logos
have been torn off. I suppose they're upset. I would be, if I had been
left like that, abandoned in the snow.

(Newsletter from Tineke Ceelen, Red Cross, Lhasa)

One of the last nomad populations on earth live in Tibet. It's not exactly an idyllic existence. There's no such thing as trekking through the mountains without a worry. The nomads belong to one of the poorest people in the world. According to official government figures, a quarter of the nomads live below the poverty line, earning less than 50 dollars a year. Adults are seldom literate and most have no access to medical care. In the northern territories, life expectancy is 46 years and one in five children dies of illness or exposure.

Whenever the nomads are not stuck in the snow, they travel around in groups of 20 families. They live in square tents. When a son marries and gets children, a smaller tent is made for him. In the summertime, the nomads sleep outside, under rough yak-hair blankets. The families erect their tents far away from each other, because the grass is not very good and the herd needs a big area to graze. The men herd the animals, while the women stay in the camp, protected by one of the men. The women weave blankets and work on the hides. The decision to go to the next place is taken by all the families together. Even in good times, the nomads have few possessions. In their tent they have a small stove, a family altar with a Buddha statue and yak butter lamps that always burn. Then there is a small chest with precious family possessions like jewels and costumes for ceremonies.

In the north, snow disasters are common. The temperature can fall to minus 37 degrees Celsius. That's when the nomads can lose their cattle within a short period of time; sometimes as many as four million yaks die in one winter. For the nomads, this means the beginning of the end. They are completely dependent on their animals. The people eat the meat. They use the milk to make yak butter. This, in turn, is used to make tea, a bad-smelling brew that people keep offering me in Tibet. The stoves burn cow dung; hides are used for clothes and tents. Once a year, mostly during the fall, after the animals have been eating the whole summer, the nomads take a few yaks to the market. With the money they earn they can buy other necessities to get through the winter.

Nomads without yaks are immediately in danger of starvation and are unable to protect themselves against the cold. How many people die during the cold winters is always unclear. According to the Chinese press, seven people froze to death and thousands were stranded during the last snowstorm in 2008, after it snowed for 36 hours in a row. The Chinese army and the Tibetan Red Cross, later followed by foreign aid organizations, sent in trucks full of clothing and food. But aid organizations say that something fundamental has to change, as this snow disaster repeats itself every five years.

The climate is not the only factor that keeps the nomads poor. In the Chinese province of Qinghai, part of the old Northern Tibet, nomads have other problems. The herdsmen there are suffering the consequences of earlier campaigns to make them all live in one place. During the political campaigns of Mao Zedong, the nomads were forced to live in houses and work on fields. The revolutionaries tried to cultivate terraced fields, like they did in the model communes of Dazhai. But that commune was situated in the province of Shanxi, where the weather is much warmer. During the Great Leap Forward, when Mao decided that the country had to develop its heavy industry, huge numbers of trees were cut down in Qinghai. The population was forced to build dams and irrigation works instead of keeping yaks. Both the climate and the land turned out to be unsuitable for agriculture. The result of the campaigns was that Qinghai now has a giant desert. Even the national newspapers complain that this barren area is increasing in size. The authorities try to stop it by planting millions of trees. They deny that the desert is the result of disastrous political campaigns. "There never were trees in Qinghai. They were never cut down to use as fuel in steel furnaces. We never did that there," one official says.

The provincial authorities state that many nomads have themselves to blame for their poverty. They would keep too many yaks, which leads to overgrazing and erosion. Then there are the environmental problems. Local scientists say that Qinghai is also a victim of global warming, and that the Western industrial countries are to blame for this.

But the authorities do admit that there is a problem which they have tried to solve in the last ten years. Last year, Chinese media reported that 80 percent of the herdsmen will be moved into permanent brick houses by 2010. Last year alone, 300,000 farmers and herders were moved under the government-led "comfortable housing program." The five-year housing project started in 2006 and aims to build solid homes for 220,000 families.

According to the Chinese media, the nomads see this as a happy occasion. "I only spent 18,000 yuan (US$2,647) on the construction of my new house, and the rest, totaling more than 40,000 yuan, was all granted by the government," China's Xinhua news agency cited Drolkar, a resident of the Yamda Village near Lhasa, as saying.

The rights group Human Rights Watch, however, painted a very different picture of the proceedings. They reported that the nomads were forced to pay for their dwellings themselves and that, in order to come up with the money, they had to slaughter herds of yaks, sheep and goats. Government officials were giving minimal compensation. The group appealed to Beijing to stop the resettlements until a review system was put in place. They quote an unhappy nomad: "They are destroying our Tibetan (herder) communities by not letting us live in our area and thus wiping out our livelihood completely."

The report went on, "Many Tibetan herders have been required to slaughter most of their livestock and move into newly built housing colonies in or near towns, abandoning their traditional way of life." The harshest efforts, the report says, took place in Sichuan's Golok region, where authorities banned grazing in 2003 and required nomads to sell their cattle and move into newly built townships. Here Human Rights Watch cited a Tibetan, "Even if we become town dwellers and try to do business, we don't have the education or the experience to succeed. We don't even know how to live from farming. So in future we will face great difficulties."

Rinzindorje, the lone man I meet on the grasslands around Lhasa, is a nomad with a house. If government policy is carried out correctly, most of the nomads will soon live like he does. In the winter he stays in his house, and during the warm months he treks around with his animals. The children stay in the village, attend school and have access to a clinic if they're sick. He can hitch a ride on the back of a truck if he wants to go to Lhasa. With the settlements for the nomads, a way of life is forever disappearing, but I didn't hear anyone complain. It can't be too good to spend your winters frozen in the snow.

RINZINDORJE, THE SETTLED NOMAD

It's not easy to find nomads around Lhasa, especially if you have a driver who doesn't feel like going very far. After an hour, he stops at a few tents, visibly relieved that there are any at all. Children with dirty faces and snotty noses come running over a plank that serves as a home-made bridge. They ask for candy first and a picture of the Dalai Lama second. But the people who live in these tents aren't nomads. They say that they own land and farm it. As soon as we get back into the car, the driver starts to explain that as long as there is snow, like now, we're not going to find any herdsmen. He wants to stop at someone's house, but I want to talk to someone who at least lives in a tent. Finally a small black dot appears on the horizon. We drive over the arid grassland towards a solitary man. We're a Westerner and two Tibetans who park their fancy car right in front of a small tent in the middle of nowhere. The man doesn't even look surprised. Rinzindorje wears an old tracksuit and sneakers under his traditional coat. He has just finished building a wall with stones that were lying around. The wall is to keep the first baby goats of the season. Rinzindorje is a wealthy man.

"I'm 53 years old now and this year I own 120 sheep and 40 yaks. My parents were also nomads; we have lived like this for generations. I inherited my first yaks from my parents, but then the leaders started communes, and we had to give them all up. Some years later, they switched to the family contract system, and we got our animals back. And that's how it went. If nobody gets sick, I sell two yaks a year. I use the money to buy grain for the winter. We don't have any savings, we have just enough to make ends meet.

"I just got here. My son and my wife are still further on. They are with one of the sheep, which is delivering a lamb. They'll join me tonight. This tent, and the four lambs and all these things, I carried on my back, how else? We are going to stay in this place for two months. In fact I live over there, but the grass is bad in that area, so we're moving here with the tent. I have a house now. In winter we live in the house, but when the grass is not good we move out here with our tents. I have a wife and five kids. My eldest will join me here, the others stayed at home.

"All the children we had survived. When they are sick, we take them to the district doctor. If they have a serious illness, he sends them to the hospital in Lhasa. You have to pay for that, first a guarantee of 2,000 yuan and the rest of the bill later. Every time someone has to go to the hospital, we sell a yak. Last year I was sick myself, I was in the hospital for 27 days. There was something wrong with my liver, I don't know what, and I had swollen ankles. Right now, my daughter is in hospital. They said at first that she also had some illness of the liver, but now they're talking about a problem with her brain. It seems to be serious; she has been there for 17 days and there is no improvement. If we sell a yak to pay the bill, we get 6,000 yuan. It also depends on the time of year. In spring the yaks are too skinny and you can't sell them for that much money. When someone is sick in spring, we try to borrow money from other families.

"I never went to school, but my youngest son does. There is a primary school now in the village. At first the children didn't attend. The school wasn't run very well and so parents preferred to keep the children at home, so they could help with the work. Children can take care of animals. But now they are obliged to go to school for at least five years. My son has to do his exams this year. If he gets good grades, he will be able to go to another province of China and attend secondary school there. I hope he makes it, because then he'll get free clothes, food and tuition. And he will be able to find a job afterwards. I don't know what kind of job; let's see if he passes his exams first. It's not easy, the tests are difficult and the school is not that good. So I tell him to study hard. If he doesn't pass, he'll just have to help us with the animals, like the others.

"I have had a house for some years now. We sold a lot of yaks to build it. No, we didn't get any money from the government, but it is good to have a place. When you live in a tent, you have to get a new one every year, but a house lasts much longer. I don't think that we're less free either. Whenever we feel like it, we take our little tents and go where we want. We have been lucky too, because we didn't get any snow disasters here, like they have in the north. We do have droughts, but not very bad ones. This is because we live under a sacred mountain, so the gods protect us.

"I remember when the People's Army came to Tibet. We were scared in the beginning, but soon that feeling went away. No, we weren't scared of the Tibetan warriors. They were our own people, although of course there were good and bad ones. The bad ones would come and ask for food and things. In the beginning we had no contact with the Chinese soldiers, they just started to build roads. Those of us who didn't own a lot of yaks went to work for them, because you could earn money. After the soldiers, the cadres arrived. They told us that the revolution was a good thing. That's when we understood that the People's Army was good too. For the first years, we didn't know what communism was. We learned that when they started to set up the communes. They told us to live and take care of all the animals together. Those who didn't have so many yaks didn't mind, but the people with many animals were shocked when the cadres organized this system. Of course they obeyed, but nobody worked very hard. People had no sense of responsibility.

"The worst time during the Cultural Revolution was when we weren't allowed to practice our religion. We couldn't pray in front of the statues. All the Buddhas, tangkas and prayer wheels were burnt. It was terrible, we thought it was awful. We were afraid that the gods would be angry, that they would punish us because we had destroyed the statues. So we still prayed to ourselves, secretly. But we couldn't refuse the revolution either, we were more frightened of the Red Guards. Yes, they were all Tibetans; I never saw a Chinese Red Guard.

"We were hungry in that time; there wasn't a lot of food. But nobody died of starvation. In 1981, I heard that they were introducing a new system, the one with individual contracts. So we went to the district leader and asked if we could implement that, and he agreed. We divided up the yaks among the families. The contract system works well. If there are problems, people try to solve them.

"I know that the Dalai Lama lives in India, because he ran away after a rebellion in Lhasa. He is our religious leader. If he was here, he would be able to help us with our problems and sorrows. Traditionally we believe that the Dalai Lama is the sun, and the Panchen Lama the moon. The

Communist Party is good too. Life nowadays is better. Long ago, there were no roads and there were no cars. To go on a pilgrimage to Lhasa was just a dream. You had to walk for many days, and who had time for that? It's a lot easier now, you just ask for a ride on a truck.

"If the party policy doesn't change, then I would like the party to stay on, together with the Dalai Lama. If the Dalai Lama had stayed, we wouldn't have been so developed. We were quite a weak country at that time. I don't know if the party is planning to change policy and what it is they do. We don't have electricity, so no TV either, and I can't read newspapers. Once in a while we have a political meeting in the village. During the times of the communes, we used to have one every day, but nowadays we just have one every few months. The last one was in February, before the Tibetan New Year. They always talk about the law, that you shouldn't steal and that you should be honest. And you're not allowed to shout slogans, like those that say Tibet should be independent. The Central Government says that it is impossible for Tibet to become independent, as we are part of China. They tell us to fight the separatists.

"In our village we have a leader. He's elected by the people. The cadres came to the village one day and told us to choose a leader. That was right after the Cultural Revolution. I'm not sure how the election process works, I don't go to those kinds of meetings; no time. I always send one of my sons. Is the village leader a good man? Excuse me, but I really have to get back to work. My wife and son are about to arrive and I still have a lot to do. They will bring the newborn lamb, and we'll have to take care of it. You know how important the animals are."

4.

ESCAPE TO A DESERTED MOUNTAIN

There are separatists in the Bank of China? I can imagine them in the temples, but in the Chinese bank? Pro-independence bank tellers who secretly channel money to the underground opposition movement? My imagination is running away with me. In any case, in the Bank of China in Lhasa, the authorities are trying to make sure no one gets any ideas. One clerk is monotonously reading out an impressively long document. She does this while the others just keep working. That way, no one loses any time and I'm sure everyone knows exactly what the document says anyway. "Abide by the laws. Do not participate in separatist activities that propagate the so-called independence of Tibet. Tibet is an indivisible part of the motherland," she drones through the echoing hall. When her throat gets dry, another colleague takes over the indoctrination job, using the same inexpressive voice. The others don't seem to be listening at all.

The clerk helping me is too busy overcoming difficulties in getting me some cash from my credit card. I have to pay the bill of the Ministry of Foreign Affairs. The bank teller doesn't believe that a driver's license can serve as an identification card. He wants my passport. Our driver comes to help me. His ID says that he works for the Foreign Ministry, and that seems to open all doors, even the ones to the safe.

There are indoctrination attempts everywhere in Lhasa. Everyone seems to receive lessons in "patriotic behavior." And the authorities don't seem to trust anyone. You can feel the tension, and the us-against-them thinking everywhere. "Sometimes, there is a rumor that you're not allowed to go on the street after 11 p.m.," one foreigner living in Lhasa says. "I still go, because I'm not going to adhere to a curfew that isn't officially announced. So I walk around all by myself." Another foreigner saw how one day a table was put on the street and some prisoners were judged in public. It's a crime to complain to foreigners. And if a Tibetan has been in contact with a stranger, and this person then goes on to complain publicly, the Tibetan can end up in jail. An American congressman once decided to carry out his own personal fact-finding mission in Tibet. He went on a tourist visa and kept his political identity hidden. Once back in the United States, he told the media expansively about the dire situation of human rights in the region. The Chinese were furious. "How can someone who doesn't know anything about Tibet see so many human rights violations in three days?" the Chinese press wrote. But it was the hotel owner who had rented a room to the congressman who was sanctioned. He wasn't allowed to receive any foreigners for six months, and that while he probably had no idea of the secret intentions of his guest.

These kind of stories make me decide that I don't want to visit Tibet secretly and unofficially. I'd prefer to wait for a year than go as a tourist and bring anyone I talk to in danger. Once in Lhasa, I also don't look for dissidents. I don't have the feeling that anyone is watching me or restricting my movements, but again, why endanger people when I can find enough refugees in India, in the community of Tibetan exiles?

The Indian diplomats in Beijing are not very pleased to give a visa to a foreign journalist who wants to write about Tibetans. "You know that this is a very sensitive issue," the embassy man says. I answer that I've lived in China for ten years, and that I'm obviously not an anti-China activist. The diplomats make me sign a paper on which I declare that my articles will not be published in local newspapers and that I won't make a movie. A week later I'm on the airplane.

It's far, through the inferno of New Delhi, where I put on a face like a thundercloud to scare off unwanted attention because people told me it's not safe for a lone blonde woman to travel through India. That turns out to be an exaggeration. A little information about my husband and children at home, and I get respectful treatment everywhere I go. I take the train to a small mountain town and, together with two other travelers I meet on the way, hire a car to take us to Dharamsala. The Dalai Lama and his followers live in a tiny town even higher up, called McLeod.

In this small town and its surroundings, about 30,000 Tibetans have settled. They have built their own mini-country. The first inhabitants followed the Dalai Lama in 1959, after the anti-Chinese riots in Lhasa. The Indian government gave the Tibetan refugees this deserted mountaintop which used to be a summer camp for British colonials. The Brits left a church called St. John in the Wilderness. In the beginning, the exiles weren't sure if they should build houses, as they thought they would be returning to Tibet soon. But then the Cultural Revolution started, and all contact with Tibet was lost. So the Tibetans ended up building a school, a hospital, a temple and even a parliament.

Nowadays the old town is a booming tourist destination. The Tibetans make a living by running hotels and shops where they sell souvenirs and "Free Tibet" T-shirts. The guests are a colorful throng of Westerners. Many are dressed in Indian batik and have rings through their noses, others wear Tibetan monk's robes. They come to the Tibetans for meditation or to find other ways of reaching higher spiritual states. The Israeli youth that I meet on the train is seeking "freedom." He started working immediately after his study and now feels that he missed something. The other traveler, a tough-looking Brit who is a guide, comments, "Yes, lots of Israelis here. They come after their military service to get rid of all the shit in their heads."

The Westerners are kindly received by the Tibetans. One man suggested that the Tibetans need to recycle, so now you can also buy homemade paper. Some Western environmentalists started a green campaign, which was embraced by the Dalai Lama. The Tibetans aren't the only ones who do good business; the tourists have also attracted the Indians from the region. They sell food by the side of the road, or beg. The begging girls who walk around with babies on their hips have discovered that the Westerners who don't want to give money are willing to buy them food. But the economic success of the immigrants also breeds jealousy. In 1997 the local population burned down a Tibetan's house. The Dalai Lama threatened to move and the locals promised that it wouldn't happen again. They also know that without the Dalai Lama and his followers, McLeod would soon once more be a deserted mountaintop.

On one of the two dilapidated roads in the center of the village is the Reception Center for newly arrived refugees. A group of monks and a few girls sit huddled together on a bench, waiting to be interviewed. A man tells me that normally about a thousand refugees a year arrive here, but this number doubles after each campaign or riot. Pemba, a skinny 16-year-old monk, is leaning on a small table. "It's like a dream here," he says. "Look at all those pictures of His Holiness." Here in India, Pemba will be placed in a monastery that bears the same name as the one he left in Tibet.

The refugees arrive in all kinds of ways. Some, like Gundun Tenzin in the next story, go to other countries first. Many walk for weeks in the direction of Nepal. With frozen limbs they arrive at the Reception Center for refugees there. Others follow a simpler road. They buy permission to take the bus to the border, and are then smuggled across by Nepalese traders. All escape routes cost at least a few hundred dollars, so the road to India is not for the poor.

At the end of the road, past the temple of the Dalai Lama and then another half-hour's hike down, is the Information Office. An arriving journalist like me gets helped immediately. Within no time, they arrange four interviews for the next day and a young man called Karma comes with me to translate. Karma studied in Norway. He takes me to people who were recently jailed and tortured, and to others who fled because they just didn't like the system.

In McLeod the authorities-in-exile give you all their figures. They state that since the Chinese invasion of Tibet, 1.2 million Tibetans have died. Some were executed, others starved. The Chinese media deny these claims, of course, but the refugees say that they base their figures on internal documents. There you can read, for instance, that after the revolt in 1959, between 10,000 and 15,000 Tibetans were killed in three days.

The exiles are not the only ones to claim atrocities. The Panchen Lama reported these cruel punishments to the Chinese authorities in one of his last speeches in 1987. He stated, "If there was a film made on all the atrocities perpetrated in Qinghai province, it would shock the viewers. In the Golok area, many people were killed and their dead bodies rolled down the hill into a big ditch. The soldiers told the family members and relatives of the dead people that they should all celebrate since the rebels had been wiped out. They were even forced to dance on the dead bodies. Soon after, the family members and relatives were also machine-gunned. They were all buried there."

Tibet's second Lama pressed the Chinese government to punish those who had carried out these acts. He warned that if the government didn't ensure that the Tibetans were happy, the trouble would never end. "We should make sure that the people of these nationalities are happy as part of the motherland. If this happens, they will be happy to work with the Chinese people in developing the nation. On the other hand, if you cling to the attitude that you will always rule and suppress the minority nationalities, then there will be serious problems in the future."

The Chinese government chose to continue its oppression and as a result unrest keeps popping up every few years. One of the most recent revolts took place on March 10, 2008, on the anniversary of the failed Tibetan uprising in 1959 and right before the Olympic Games in Beijing. China says 22 people died in the chaos, including five female shop assistants who burned to death in an arson attack. The Tibetan government-in-exile claims more than 200 Tibetans were killed during the riots and a further 200 were jailed in the crackdown that followed. The Chinese media blamed the Dalai Lama for organizing the revolt. The religious leader reacted by inviting Chinese government representatives to scrutinize the files and computers of the government in Dharamsala. They ignored the request.

Some things never change. Tibet went through the same series of events at the end of the 1980s. The only difference then was that riots in Lhasa took place at the same time as Chinese students demonstrated on Tiananmen Square. Both places saw the army march in to end the protests in bloodshed. But after that, the situation in China's capital improved. China nowadays is quiet, relaxed and people are busy earning money. The people can complain about their leaders, as long as they don't do this in public. They know that there is a limit, but as long as they don't start petitions or write articles attacking the government, like dissidents do, or as long as they don't set up associations that work against the authorities, they are allowed to complain. The years after Tiananmen, when everyone was afraid to speak out, are over in China. But this kind of relaxation did not take place in Lhasa. After all, the Tibetans made it clear that they would never give up. While the students in Beijing surrendered after the bloodbath on Tiananmen Square and went to work, Tibet has seen some form of demonstration every few years. Between 1987 and 1993 there were continuous riots and unrest, followed by crackdowns. But the more the Chinese authorities try to oppress the demonstrators, the more determined they get. The latest riot was one of the most widespread in decades.

Even in quiet times, Tibetans get arrested for all kinds of reasons: talking to foreign reporters, singing patriotic songs, hanging posters, or even just being in possession of the autobiography of the Dalai Lama. One person got arrested for "inciting others to wear traditional Tibetan clothes during a Chinese holiday." Sometimes people get arrested for no reason at all, the exiles report. Just like in China, dissidents can disappear without a trace and the family won't be informed. The latest famous case of a disappearing Tibetan is that of Wangdu, a 41-year-old HIV/Aids project officer with the Burnet Institute, an Australian medical non-governmental organization. Wangdu vanished in Lhasa during the 2008 protests. His family had no news from him for months, until local media reported on his conviction. That's when they found out that Wangdu was charged with passing information regarding the protest to the outside world and was sentenced to life in prison.

Chinese authorities don't always deny these claims. In 1996 a regional police chief in Tibet was convicted because he had tortured a woman, Chinese media reported. He had tied up the woman and told her, "I am the authority here. It will be of no use to report me." This says a lot about the positions of power that the local cadres have in the region. They seem to think that they can do whatever they want, and since they are far away and it is hard to control them, this is probably true. The cadres feel supported by statements from the state leaders who keep saying that the separatists need to be crushed and harshly punished.

The West by now has caught on, and 2009 actually saw some diplomatic breakthroughs for the Dalai Lama. During his visit to the European Parliament, the Dalai Lama addressed the full plenary. The Chinese were furious. They had already canceled an EU-China summit in Lyon after French president Nicolas Sarkozy held a separate meeting with the Dalai Lama in Poland.

When given an opportunity to defend themselves, the Chinese don't do so well. The answers might as well come from a tape recorder. Song

Zhu, China's most senior diplomat in Brussels, said that Tibet had been an "inalienable" part of China "since ancient times" and that in the past, Tibetans "did not have any democracy, human rights or freedom to speak of." Song, who heads China's mission to the EU, also said that until China implemented reforms in 1959, "their conditions were worse than animals and life was miserable." He said that Tibetans now enjoyed "a wide range of political rights and unprecedented fundamental human rights." Life expectancy had risen from 35 to 69, adult illiteracy had fallen from 95 percent to 4.48 percent and the region's GDP was higher than China's national average. The ambassador also insisted that Beijing "fully respects and effectively guarantees" the religious freedom of Tibetans.

But this is not what the West wants to hear. They don't care if Tibet historically was part of China or not. Western diplomats aren't pleading a case for independence; they would like to do something to ensure better treatment of the Tibetan people and bring about serious negotiations between China and the Dalai Lama. And it would help if the local cadres and police would treat the people as if they were human, as opposed to separatist enemies who need to be crushed.

GUNDUN TENZIN, THE REFUGEE

From the front of Gundun's small house in McLeod we look out over the mountains. Not long after the sun sets, a pitch-black darkness surrounds us. The friendly, skinny man with mousy hair takes out a torch and lights up my notebook. We are there for hours because Gundun has a long story to tell: from meeting the warriors in his native Tibetan village to a stint as a beggar in Bhutan to becoming leader of the refugee Reception Center in India.

"The Chinese told us that we were the oppressed ones. They gave us permission to attack anyone who had ever dominated us. But we never trusted them.

"We are from the area around Shigatse. My parents were farmers and illiterate, but they had their own kind of wisdom. They knew everything about nature. They could look at the mountains and the sky and they would tell you if the harvest would be good this year or not. I was born in 1946. We led a peaceful existence. That's what I remember most when I think of my early childhood: peace. There was no violence.

"I also remember the day the Chinese came. They had cameras and equipment to measure land and they started to assess everything, the mountains and the rivers. They camped out on a big field near our village and told us not to come close. They told us they had placed landmines around their camp.

"A few years later there was a big flood in our region. Many people lost their homes. Aid organizations from India came to help us, but later I heard that the Chinese had sent them back. They had told them they would rebuild all the dams and bridges themselves. And they did. The villagers went to build the bridge and the Chinese paid them a salary. But the dams were of poor quality. During the next storm, they all collapsed and soon we had another flood.

"In 1956 His Holiness went to visit India and on his way back he passed by our region. It was an important event in our lives, as seeing His Holiness meant good fortune. The local cadres constructed a school really fast and they put posters of Mao Zedong everywhere. We children were all put along the road, the girls holding flowers and the boys waving red flags at His Holiness.

"During that time, rumors started. People from Amdo province came and said that there were big problems there. They said that the Chinese made the rich people do dirty work and that they wanted to destroy Buddhism. Until that time, the Chinese hadn't changed many things. We heard that the Tibetans had started to resist the Chinese; even monks had left the monasteries to fight with the guerillas. They were allowed to, as the Chinese were killing us, so it was their moral obligation to fight back.

Of course monks are not allowed to use violence, so they had to leave the monastery permanently. We children also wanted to join up. We talked about it for days. But I was 12 years old and of course there was no way I would be allowed to go.

"Not until 1959 was there fighting in our village. That's when I saw that all the rumors we had heard were true. The guerillas had hidden themselves right next to our village, in the mountains. We gave them food. One of my friends, a monk, also worked for them. He told them when the Chinese were approaching. One day, he took me along on a scouting mission. We went close to the Chinese camp to see what they were doing. That day, it was quiet, but on another morning, my friend came racing through the street on his horse. About 40 soldiers, also on horseback, soon followed him. We were playing in the fields and one elder came to tell us to hide, because there was going to be a battle. But we were curious children, and hid close by in the bushes, so we could see everything.

"The riders were followed by a group of walking soldiers. They looked exhausted. You could see that they had been walking for weeks. Suddenly one of the riders came back and told them something and they all started crying. Later we heard that the guerillas had ambushed the Chinese riders and killed all of them. The man we had seen was the only survivor.

"The Chinese left and the whole night we heard cannon fire coming from the mountains. We all escaped in the opposite direction. The soldiers came back and took our houses. When the fighting was over, we started to return. As soon as we were settled in, the Chinese held a meeting in the village. They told us that we had been slaves, and that we should tell them what the masters had done to us. Some people refused to say anything bad about the masters, but others saw it as a great opportunity to seek revenge on rich people they didn't like. The Chinese said that the rich were slave owners, but later we understood that they were just normal people who disagreed with the Chinese. In this way, 30 people were arrested in our region.

"After that the land was divided. My family also got some land and a few yaks. We got whatever the Chinese couldn't take with them. We never saw the gold and jewels that the rich people had owned; they kept those for themselves. Some people in the village were very happy. But in my family, even though we hadn't been punished, we still didn't trust the revolutionaries. We saw how they also criticized good people. Apart from rich people, they had also arrested some farmers. We had to pay tax to the new authorities and when the farmers didn't have enough, they were beaten. Some had to stand up by the side of the road until they fainted. Then they were beaten and forced to stand up again.

"One day a rumor went around that all intelligent or promising children in the village would be sent to China to be educated. I was of the right age. We would become Chinese, lose our own culture and grow up to be very bad people, the elders in the village said. That's when my parents decided to flee with me. We walked for a week, hiding during the day and moving at night. There were seven of us. We were really happy when we reached the border. We thought, "Now the Chinese can't touch us any more. They can do what they want, we are free now."

"By then we had lost all our possessions as we couldn't stay with the yaks that carried our things during the crossing. The Bhutanese soldiers helped us. They let us sleep in their camp and then they told us to walk to a bigger camp. We walked again, for days, through the rain. It was terribly hot and our clothes were full of insects. In the big camp there was nothing, no food, no clothes, no tents. We made our own tents from whatever we could find. People started to get sick and die. There was no clean water and everybody had diarrhea. There was one small local hospital and every day there was a long row of Tibetans in front of the door. But we were sure that we didn't want to go back to Tibet, we didn't even think about that.

"After a few years in the camp, the situation improved. But then the Bhutanese government decided to send us to live in villages. It was their way to solve the refugee problem. We were spread all over the country so we wouldn't all live in one place. In the villages we had to take care of ourselves, nothing was done to help us. So we tried to find jobs or we begged. Later some delegates of the Dalai Lama came from India and they helped us to establish a Tibetan community. In Bhutan I taught myself a little to read and write. By then I was too old to go to school.

"In 1974 we got into trouble in Bhutan. The Tibetans were accused of plotting to kill the King. This was nonsense, the political parties were playing a game: right accused left and left accused right. The King had a Tibetan girlfriend and I think that's why they blamed the Tibetans. Some were even arrested. The politicians declared that we all had to switch to Bhutanese nationality, but 99 percent of the Tibetans refused. In 1981 almost 2,000 people got permission to go to India. We were part of this lucky group. Even nowadays the relations between Tibetans and Bhutanese are not very good. Teachers from India still can't go there to teach the Tibetan children. I think that the Bhutanese government is afraid of China.

"So that's how we ended up here. I was given a job in the refugee center. I interview the newly arrived. We receive about a thousand people a year. About three in every hundred have been in prison. The older ones, those above 30, and those who are not monks or nuns, have the hardest time. They have to find a job. They get to have an audience with His Holiness and after that we take care of them for one month. After that, they have to be ready with a house and work. There are more and more students. Some don't want to receive a Chinese education, just like me. The young ones are placed in the children's village.

"In 1993 I went back to Tibet for a visit. It was shocking to see how ignorant the villagers are. Not only are they illiterate, the people also know nothing about the world. In the old Tibet we were behind, but in the monasteries there were famous scholars. These monasteries were destroyed and the scholars are nowhere to be found. You only see beggars, many more than before. The Chinese have rebuilt the monasteries, but they're not the same. We'll never be able to get back those beautiful places of long ago.

"I asked one Tibetan cadre who works for the Chinese, "This is the ten percent that survived?" He didn't know what to answer. In the end he stammered that the destruction had been the fault of the Gang of Four, during the Cultural Revolution, and that the new government is not responsible. Of course I couldn't start political discussions with the villagers. That would have been too dangerous. I had waited months to get a visa to visit my old village. So the authorities had time enough to prepare everything. They had been told not to speak about politics with me.

"It's also impossible to help them. The only thing you are allowed to do is compliment the Chinese. I wanted to set up a project for the people, but wasn't allowed. I suggested to the local authorities that I would just provide the money and that they would manage the project, but they didn't approve. From here, being a refugee, you can't do anything. During the eighties a few Tibetans did manage to set up some aid missions, but now the Chinese don't accept this any more. You can only go back if you have the status of an "overseas Chinese", just like Chinese people who have moved to a foreign country and taken on nationality there. But who wants to be called an overseas Chinese? Under these circumstances it is no use to go back to Tibet. It won't help anybody.

"And you can't trust the Chinese. They just want to put pressure on you. They never did anything to me personally, but I see how their goals never changed. The nomads still live in traditional ways, but the cities are becoming completely Chinese. They say that is for our development, but I didn't see one educated Tibetan who was helping with the construction.

No matter what they say, they are still trying to extinguish the Tibetan culture."

BHAGDRO, THE TORTURED MONK

Bhagdro wrote a book entitled *Hell on Earth*. He shows me the front page, a picture of himself in front of the Tibetan flag. A publisher in New Delhi, sponsored by some foreign friends, published it. "I hope someone can make a movie about me," the friendly monk dreams. We are having a meal in the Indian restaurant in Dharamsala. Someone is playing very loud country and western music, and the people behind the bar refuse to turn down the volume. An American priest comes by. He says he needs to speak to Bhagdro before he leaves.

"I was released in 1991. When I came here, I was near collapse. I felt terrible and trembled all over. My nose was always bleeding because of the electric shocks they administered to my head, and I had mental problems. They treated me in a hospital in France. Mrs. Mitterrand paid the bill. The French doctors asked many questions and they took me to a quiet place. They also gave me medicine. After a few years' rest, I'm feeling better. I don't tremble any more.

"I'm from Lhasa. My parents are farmers. At home we never talked about politics. My parents were afraid that I would say something to other people and then the whole family would get into trouble. There was a school in our town, but I attended it for maybe a month. They only taught us about Mao Zedong. This was during the Cultural Revolution and the children were taught to be revolutionaries. At school they learned about Chinese policy, then the pupils would go home and ask their parents about the correct line. If the parents didn't know, the children would beat them. I've seen this with my own eyes; my cousin beat my uncle.

"The Chinese took a lot of our grain, so we didn't have much to eat. We were so poor that my sister died because of our poor living conditions.

Many people around us went begging. When I was 12, I was put to work. I had to plant trees in the hills. While we were planting away, the Chinese cut down the big trees. Every day we saw truckloads of timber pass by, so we knew they were just keeping us busy.

"When I was young I knew nothing about His Holiness. I didn't even know he existed, I only knew about the Panchen Lama. I did realize that we were different from Chinese people, as we saw how they would punish Tibetans. And of course there was the difference in language. In 1983, their policy towards religion became a little more liberal. The Chinese kept saying that God was a bad spirit, but at the same time, they started to rebuild the monasteries. I think that was because of pressure by the Dalai Lama on foreign countries.

"I decided to enter a monastery, mostly because I was hungry. I knew that in a monastery I would get food. My father had been a monk when he was young, so he was happy that I went. But it wasn't simple. First I had to wait until I was 18 and I had to find a teacher. After that, I went through many formalities. The local authorities had to give their consent. I had to be a Marxist and they made me sign a document. I don't know what it said, as I didn't know how to read at that time.

"When I entered the Ganden monastery, one of the biggest in Tibet, I couldn't start studying Buddhism right away. The monastery had been destroyed and we spent a year building it up again. In the monastery I saw my first picture of the Dalai Lama. I didn't even know what a photograph was, so I was amazed that someone could draw so well. Later on I also saw foreigners with cameras for the first time. They were blond, and we thought they were from India. They wanted to take a picture of us, but we were afraid those strange machines they were holding would shoot us, so we ran away.

"I started my religious study a year later and so then I learned about the Dalai Lama. The monks couldn't say too much, because there were spies in the monasteries everywhere. We couldn't talk about Tibetan independence or even show a picture of His Holiness. The Chinese did give us posters of Mao Zedong and Deng Xiaoping to hang, and they told us that these were powerful people. They also showed us movies about their heroic deeds. But I knew they were all Chinese; bad people who lied a lot. So I was very confused. Nowadays, in Tibet, there are still many people who are puzzled like that.

"Then I met an American tourist who gave me His Holiness' book, *My Land and My People*, in Tibetan. I went to my room and secretly read it, cried, and then I knew everything. As soon as I was finished, I became active. I started by hanging the Mao posters upside down, or stabbing them with a knife. I read the book in 1987, right before the first demonstrations happened. The Chinese police station on the Barkhor, in front of the Jokhang temple, was attacked. In October there was another demonstration by monks from the Sera monastery. That was three hours away from us. We wanted to go there, but the Chinese stopped us. They surrounded our monastery with 25 army jeeps. They told us that the monks in the other two monasteries were bad people. "You are good ones," they said. They wanted to give us money because we "supported" them. Every monk would get 70 yuan. We refused to take the money, which they saw as a form of protest. They always had this strategy: at first they would be very nice and when that didn't work, they would become aggressive. They started yelling that they had prisons enough to lock us up in and that they could also shoot us all if they wanted. They raised their guns to scare us.

"Then, in March 1988, there was the Mon Lap ceremony. The Chinese had invited all these Westerners. They wanted to show them that there was religious freedom in Tibet. But the square in front of the Jokhang temple was filled with secret police. Some were even dressed up as monks. Guns were pointed at us everywhere, through the windows of opposite buildings. You call that religious freedom? Chinese propaganda is all lies.

"At first we refused to participate in the ceremony. The Chinese sent buses to the monasteries and threatened to fire all the high lamas if we didn't go. So then we decided to sacrifice our lives for Tibet. We were going to give those Westerners a message by demonstrating. At eight o'clock at night we started our ceremony. As soon as it was finished, we started the revolt. We sang "Tibet is independent," burned down Chinese shops and overturned the army trucks. Immediately the Chinese started shooting at us. One girl was shot right in front of me; others were covered in blood. The police started to push monks from the roof of the Jokhang temple. After that all the monks' rooms were plundered.

"I was shot in the leg. Around three o'clock in the afternoon, many people were arrested, 11 from our monastery. They were thrown like cattle into the army trucks. I managed to escape but I couldn't go back to the monastery. A few peddlers, who had been selling goods on the Barkhor, helped me. They dressed me up as a woman, and so I escaped, but the Chinese knew my name. They had filmed me throwing stones at a Chinese photographer, so they put a ransom on my head of 1,000 yuan. When that didn't work, as no one betrayed me, they started to threaten my parents. So in the end I gave myself up as I didn't want my parents to get into trouble.

"What happened then… do you really want me to tell you all that? I really don't like to talk about it. Here is an article, can you quote that?

After my arrest the officials abused me, kicked me and beat me with rifle butts. My handcuffs were self-tightening and they cut through my wrists. I was put in a truck and taken to Ganden Monastery where again Chinese soldiers and the Work Investigation Unit kicked, slapped and beat me with rifle butts all over my body. Blood was streaming out of my nose and mouth.

While I was being taken back to Lhasa, the vehicle stopped by heavy forest and I was whipped with tree branches and beaten with electric cattle prods. I was seriously injured due to these beatings. I was then taken to Gutsa Prison where I was chained with new handcuffs and manacled and hung upside down at the gate of the prison compound for one whole day. For another week I was kept standing still and I was also made to stand naked in freezing cold weather as icy water was poured over me.

During interrogation, I was accused of being involved in the killing of a Chinese policeman during the demonstration and was told to give names of others who took part in the demonstration. They also wanted me to say that Tibet is not an independent country. I steadfastly refused to comply with their demands and the Chinese officials started beating me with electric cattle prods on my head, mouth and on my chest close to the heart which sent me into fits of spasms. When I lost consciousness they would pour cold water over me to revive me. I started vomiting blood from the beatings. In addition to the cattle prod, they whipped me with iron chains, kicked me and beat me with rifle butts. They also made me lie down flat on my stomach on a table with my head resting on my face while they stamped on my back with their heavy boots.

For seven days I was not provided anything to eat and drink. Unable to stand the hunger and thirst, I drank the turbid laundry water from the drain and when I saw bits of food floating on its surface I crouched down and ate them. Later they put me in a cell and provided me with a little food but it was such a small amount that it could not satisfy my hunger. Unable to stand the gnawing hunger I took cotton out of my quilt and ate it and drank my own urine. For one month I was subjected to intense interrogation, always accompanied by torture, and as a result I began to suffer from failing memory and heart problems. Many other political prisoners suffered as I did. Sonam Wangdu, charged along with me, had his

back broken from severe beatings; Tsering Nyima lost his hearing;
and Lobsang Tenzin is in a similar condition. I was kept in Gutsa
Detention Center for one whole year.
    (Fearless Voices: Accounts of Tibetan Former Political Prisoners)

"Look," Bhagdro says. "Here is a picture of me during the trial. Five of us were judged at the same time. One got the death penalty, but that was later converted to life in prison. During the trial I was wearing normal clothes. In jail, we weren't allowed to wear monk's robes. Before the trial, I was warned that I shouldn't say that I had been beaten, but I think it was easy to see, I was really ill. I wasn't allowed to defend myself either, as I had refused to cooperate with the authorities. I had refused to sign a confession for a crime I hadn't committed. They accused me of killing a Chinese soldier, but there was no proof whatsoever. Because of that lack of proof, I was sentenced to just three years.

"The people who tortured me were just bad through and through. They want to destroy our culture and they have a very bad ideology. Of course I tried to see them as human beings. I thought that, since they were people like you and me, they would understand us one day. We would just have to explain things, but that didn't happen. Even now, I still try to see them as humans. We can go around killing them, but that won't bring us independence. I remember how sick some Chinese soldiers were. Sometimes they were shaking from the cold and you could see that they also lived in dire circumstances.

"Before I was released, my friends in prison told me I had to go to India instead of trying to organize further riots in Tibet. We decided that I should tell the world what happened in Tibet. After my release, I wasn't able to go back into the monastery anyway, I had been expelled. So I got a ride on a truck to Mount Everest and from there we walked for almost three months. This was difficult for many people, but for me it was horrible. I could hardly walk straight, I had such stomach aches.

"One day the situation in Tibet will change, but it will take a long time and it will be difficult. The Chinese are becoming stronger all the time. Look at the student demonstrations on Tiananmen Square, they were never repeated. The truth is on our side and the international community knows everything about Tibet. But they still shake hands with the Chinese. You are a journalist; you need to tell your government that it follows the wrong policy. They shouldn't trade with China. It's no use that the West helps the Chinese to become rich. I know that we live in the age of entertainment and business, and that people are not really interested in our struggle. When India detonates a nuclear bomb, the United Nations holds a special meeting, but they never do that for us.

"In the end, only the Chinese can change themselves. In England I stood outside the Chinese embassy every day for four hours. I kept that up for four months. I didn't want the Chinese to forget what they had done to me, and I wanted to ask the British people to support me. Some English and American people came to stand with me; others brought me food. But the Chinese just ignored me, they looked irritated and didn't say a word. Tibet support groups and other friends pay for my travels around the world. I have many friends in Hollywood, like Richard Gere and other actors who play in movies about Tibet.

"My parents are still in Tibet. I don't know what has happened to them, now that I go around the world demonstrating. But I think to myself: they are one family and the protests help the fate of six million Tibetan people."

MARJA KOOLEN, THE WESTERN EYEWITNESS

"I worked in Lhasa for a year and a half for all kinds of organizations. I came in 1986. The atmosphere was very tense. From 1987 and especially in 1988 there were constant demonstrations. Most of the time there was a small group of monks or nuns who walked around with the Tibetan flag or shouted slogans for Tibetan independence. Every time this happened, the police would appear in army trucks and all demonstrators would be thrown in the back and taken away.

"One day, in the summer of 1988, we were sitting in a restaurant next to the Barkhor, when all of a sudden we heard a loud bang. We ran outside. On the square everybody was standing flat against the walls, terrified. In the middle there were two soldiers with machine guns. They were slowly, and very threateningly, turning around and pointing their guns at the petrified people. Later we found out that three nuns had staged a demonstration again, and this was the response.

"In September of that year, there had been a riot during which the police station was torched. In December it was the 40th anniversary of the Universal Declaration of Human Rights. The Chinese expected a demonstration that day. They wanted to teach the Tibetans a lesson, so they were waiting for a provocation. As soon as demonstrators appeared, the Chinese opened fire, without hesitation and without warning.

"That day, I'm walking around the Jokhang temple with a few friends. It's really crowded. All of a sudden, some Tibetans start pointing and yelling. A group of about 20 youngsters passes, one of whom is carrying a Tibetan flag. They look very frightened and are silent, no slogans, nothing, only the flag. They don't provoke anybody and there is no way you could call it a revolt. Immediately a whole cordon of soldiers arrives and we can't see anything any more.

"In such a situation, everybody has his or her own reaction. One of my friends walks to the front to see what will happen to the demonstrators. I try to walk away. But before I have a chance to turn around, I have been hit. I feel the pain first, and hear the gunshot later. It's as if someone is setting off firecrackers. It takes a while before I realize that they're really shooting, you don't expect that. The crowd that we are part of is not demonstrating at all. But the soldiers shoot straight into the crowd. You can imagine, just in the time it takes me to turn around, they're shooting already. That didn't even take a minute.

"I get up and start running. I try to find a place to hide in one of the smaller alleys. There is an upturned table, but behind it there is a group of hiding people and no place for me. I don't know what to do, so together with an old man, who is shot in the leg, I go sit in front of the table. Then a group of soldiers runs into the alley, firing their guns in all directions. I realize that if we stay where we are, we will die. The soldiers are shooting at random, without seeing their victims. The old man and I look each other in the eye and we both yell at the same time "Run!" We start to sprint. The old man falls; I don't know what happened to him. I run at least 30 meters in front of a group of shooting soldiers. There is no one in the alley any more, but they keep on charging. I can hear the bullets flying by my head.

"I run into another alley and knock on someone's door. There is a courtyard and it's also full of people, many of them wounded. People are crying. On the street the soldiers have started to pick out anyone who looks like a participant in the demonstrations. They are throwing them into army trucks left and right. I tell the Tibetans in the house, "Please go find me a foreigner. It doesn't matter who." So they come back with some of my friends.

"My friends try to take me to the hospital, but that building is heavily guarded. I hang onto one of the boys and we pretend to be a loving couple. This way, we think, we won't look like we just came from the riots. At that time, I thought we were properly disguised, but one of my friends took a picture of us and later I saw how ridiculous our plan was. I was dressed in a pink down jacket that had blood all over it.

"Once inside, I don't get treatment, but a cross-examination. The Tibetan doctors are sent out. The police also try to throw out my friends, but they literally hold onto the side of the bed, so they can't be pulled out the door. A Chinese man spends five hours asking me questions, while playing with a gun. I refuse to answer.

"A Chinese doctor appears and starts to examine my wound. Then he says, "This is very serious. If we don't operate on you right now, you will die." But I don't want to let these people operate on me, especially not with total anesthesia. They take me to the operating room anyway. There I am, with a needle in my arm, and I decide that I don't trust this. So I try to get up and say, "Let me go home." In the end they give me a local anesthesia and one of my friends, who is a nurse, holds my hand while they clean my wound.

"After the operation the two policemen come back and take me. My friends are sitting in the hallway and see how I am carted away. They push the policemen to the side and roll me into the elevator. The Chinese run to a lower floor and press the elevator button there, so the door opens and the policemen pull me out again. Downstairs there is a reception room filled with patients waiting for treatment. It must have been a strange sight, a bed with a foreigner in it and all those people pulling at it. The doctor comes again to say that if I don't stay in the hospital, I will die. So my friends and I all get pushed into a room again.

"Then they start a good-cop bad-cop routine, except the nurses perform it. First someone comes in to state that I am a criminal and should be happy to be treated so well. Then a nurse comes in and says that I can trust her; that we're like sisters. I keep on repeating, "I don't want to stay here," but they lock the door. Then a whole group of little Chinese men appear with cameras and try to take pictures of me. My friends become so mad that they literally throw the men out of the room. One starts to beat up this photographer with a broom, everyone is furious. The only thing that I'm thinking is, "If I want to leave Tibet alive, I'll have to get out of this hospital first."

"In the end they give in and we go back to my hotel room in the Holiday Inn. The room has been searched and they took my things, my diary, letters, pictures and books. There were some beautiful pictures I had taken during my trips. I suppose the Public Security Bureau is enjoying them. We try to buy a ticket out, but the front desk already has a message that we're not allowed to leave. We can't call anybody either, not even the Dutch embassy. Strange enough, others are able to call us. And the international media have discovered that a foreigner has been shot, so five minutes later I'm talking to the BBC. I still don't understand why they didn't prevent this from happening. The media keep on calling the whole week. The Dutch embassy calls me in the end too. They are upset with the authorities because no one informed them about my case.

"Meanwhile we hear all these lies on the state radio about me. They say that I'm a spy for the Dalai Lama, that I was holding hands with the person who was carrying the Tibetan flag, that I had an affair with a monk, that I had been wearing Tibetan clothes. The Dutch embassy, at the same time, is trying to get the authorities to give me back my passport. They keep promising that this will happen the next day, but it keeps getting postponed. In the end, four policemen come with a scroll. They say I have to sign it, so I ask them to translate. The first sentence says "I am a criminal. I have broken the law of the People's Republic of China." I say, "You can stop. There's no way I'm putting my signature here."

"They answer, "Then you won't get your passport back."

"Me: "I have a list. I don't only want my passport; there are also my books, pictures and diary. And I want an apology from the authorities, my medical expenses paid." I keep adding to the list, they look at me flabbergasted. A situation like that gives you energy and you become brave. You don't let yourself be intimidated and you don't give in or do what they tell you.

"I never got my things back, just my passport, and then I was allowed to leave. My friends already had their tickets, with deportation orders for the next day. At the airport we were checked – no, turned inside out describes it better. When I arrived in Hong Kong, an enormous crowd of journalists greeted me. I was sent to an old military doctor, who at first couldn't believe my story. When he looked at the X-rays, he said, "I've never seen such a wound. You should have been killed." The bullet went in the front and came out in the back and didn't touch any organs. It went past the heart and lungs and even missed nerves and bones. I still have a scar right next to my shoulder blade. I never really told this to the media, because I didn't want my family in Holland to worry. My mother called me in Lhasa and said, "I read in the paper that it's just a flesh wound, so I suppose you're OK?" So I left it at that.

"My Tibetan friends believe that a special spirit protected me and that none of this is a coincidence. I merely felt responsibility. I saw that this was a good occasion to tell the world what had happened. I got out because I happened to have a Western passport and because I had survived. So I immediately thought: I can use this story as a human rights testimony. I sometimes wonder what would have happened if I had died. The story wouldn't have lasted that long.

"Because of my story, and through the work of other people, the Netherlands was the first country to say anything about the situation in Tibet at the United Nations since 1965. I was really happy about that. They never asked for apologies, but in the end the statement of the Dutch government was worth much more.

"I gave testimony at the Commission for Human Rights at the United Nations. The Chinese delegation was very aggressive. When I went to the toilet, a few members were waiting for me outside. "Be careful what you do. China is a powerful country," they said. As a reaction to my stories they first declared that no one had shot at me. After that, they changed the story: the soldiers had used rubber bullets. But that was hard to keep up, considering my wound. In the end they stated that they had indeed fired at me, but that was because I had been wearing Tibetan clothes. Nonsense of course, and I had a picture to prove that I wore a pink down jacket and jeans that day. But more important than that was the implication. It was OK to shoot at Tibetans? In 1990 an independent subcommittee of the UN passed a resolution against China. This was after testimony from me and from students who had survived the uprising on Tiananmen Square. The Chinese were stunned; they didn't know what was happening. The resolution never passed at the official Committee for Human Rights. But until 1992, Tibet got a lot of high-level support.

"I never went back to China or Tibet. It's now been many years. I wasn't really traumatized. After it all happened, I talked a lot with the media, and that helped. There was just this one occasion when it all came back. One day I'm walking on the street in Amsterdam and I hear a loud bang. Without thinking, I jump behind a car, until I realize that this time, I'm just hearing firecrackers."

5.

FLEEING FOR EDUCATION

Shesrab Nyima considers himself a lucky man; not just because he escaped the fate of being a serf – he was born after the liberation – but also because he is able to dedicate his time to the preservation of his ethnic culture, which was neglected prior to the 1950s. Born into a poor family in Luhuo county in the Garze Tibetan autonomous prefecture of Sichuan province in 1955, Shesrab Nyima is vice-president of Beijing's Central University of Nationalities, which studies the 56 ethnic groups of the world's most populous country. But Shesrab Nyima is not the only scholar in his family: his four siblings all graduated from university, which is a rare feat for people of their generation.

"My mother, who worked as a maid, was given the chance to go to school by the government after the liberation, and she began to understand the power of knowledge. Later, despite poverty and difficulties, she insisted that all five of her children went to school," Shesrab Nyima said. "My siblings and I were very lucky to have been able to take advantage of the new education policy."

Shesrab Nyima was among the first group of children in his county to go to middle school. Prior to the 1960s, there was no comprehensive education system in Tibetan-populated regions. Also, in 1978, he was able to take part in the reintroduced national college entrance examinations for colleges, which had been halted during the "cultural revolution" (1966-76). Shesrab Nyima was exempted from school fees and enjoyed extra benefits as he was from an ethnic minority. For example, coming from a Tibetan family meant he did not have to work in the development of rural areas, but instead was offered the chance to study at a teaching college after leaving middle school. "My success and the success of my siblings epitomizes the development of education in the region," he said.

(Wu Jiao, *China Daily*, April 23, 2008)

"One time, on the way to the toilet, a Chinese student tripped over me accidentally. He went up to a Chinese teacher and told him that I had made him fall. The teacher made me get some sand and he mixed the sand with pieces of broken glass and water. This muddy mixture was then spread out on the floor. I had to kneel for one hour in this mud. The glass cut into my knees and into my feet. It hurt very much and my knees were bleeding. The teacher told me that if I moved because it hurt I would have to kneel for an even longer time. I still dream about it. ... I stayed in hospital for four weeks due to some infection. Another Tibetan boy had received the same punishment ... The glass had gone all the way to the bone and infected it and later the boy's leg had to be amputated from the knee down."

(*The Next Generation*, Tibetan Government-in-Exile, Dharamsala)

It's not easy to be young and wanting to get ahead when you're Tibetan. Chances are that there is no school in your village. And if there is one, you might have to learn Chinese first. The Chinese authorities have claimed for over 50 years now that they give the Tibetan people a chance to be educated. But the situation in Tibet is bad enough for many parents to send their children by themselves over the mountains to India, so that they can study. Fewer travel restrictions make this possible, but even then, most children have to be smuggled out. Children who come without parents are housed in nine Tibetan Children's Villages. By now there are over 16,000 youngsters who have followed this path.

This doesn't mean that there are no schools in Tibet. From the beginning, the Chinese authorities sent groups of poor and formerly oppressed to schools in China and made them into party cadres. But then the Cultural Revolution broke out and, just like in China itself, that meant that a whole generation didn't get any education at all.

Nowadays schools are built at a high speed in the region. The Chinese media try to show that the government is doing everything it can to bridge the gap. It publishes a dazzling amount of figures on the subject. "Educational and cultural levels have been noticeably improved. Now in Tibet, there are 884 primary schools, 94 high schools and 1,237 teaching stations, with a total enrollment of 547,000. The illiteracy rate has fallen from more than 95 percent in old Tibet to the present 4.76 percent. The enrollment rate for school-age children has risen from 2 percent in old Tibet to the present 98.2 percent, and the enrollment rate for junior high schools has reached 90.97 percent, basically ensuring free nine-year compulsory education. At present, there are 14 senior high schools and nine schools with both junior and senior high school education, with the enrollment rate for senior high schools hitting 42.96 percent; seven secondary vocational schools, with students totaling 19,000 in 2007; and six colleges and universities, with students numbering 27,000 and an enrollment rate of 17.4 percent." (Protection and Development of Tibetan Culture, *China Daily*, 2008).

It goes on: "There are 30,652 teachers in primary and high schools, colleges and universities, among whom teachers of the Tibetan or other ethnic minority groups account for more than 80 percent. Throughout the country, 33 schools have classes especially for Tibetan students, including 19 junior high schools, 12 senior high schools and two teacher-training schools. In addition, 53 key senior high schools in inland

China enroll students from Tibet. By the end of June 2008, a total of 34,650 Tibetan students had been admitted to these schools, and at present the number of Tibetan students has reached 17,100. The higher education admission rate of these Tibetan classes in inland China has exceeded 90 percent. Meanwhile, over 90 inland colleges and universities have admitted students from Tibet, with a total of 5,200 students still studying, and 15,000 having already graduated. Large numbers of highly educated Tibetans, including some with PhDs and MAs, as well as scientists and engineers, have become a major force in promoting Tibet's development."

So why are parents still sending their children on a two-week walk through snow and ice to get an education? The exiles in India state that the Chinese authorities are not interested in educating the Tibetans. After all, it's easier to control a herdsman on the grasslands than a university student. For this reason, the Dalai Lama followers dismiss every *China Daily* article about educational development. They wrote their own book, entitled *The Next Generation*, in which the situation of schooling in the region is explained in detail.

According to the refugees, China never planned to educate the Tibetans. The schooling of the first poor was purely politically motivated. "As was the case in other parts of China, the spread of Communist ideology continued throughout the 1950s and 1960s and it became a major goal to send Tibetan children to study in China. In the eastern part of Tibet especially, many parents were forced to send their children, including infants, to China for further studies. At the same time, some went to China voluntarily and were kept in special schools which enjoyed good facilities. Education, however, remained an indoctrination into Communist ideology, and often included curriculum that taught that the Tibetan tradition was backward."

The Chinese immediately react to these statements by saying that in the old Tibet there were no schools at all. The information of the Tibetans in

India contradicts this statement. They say that in the old Tibet there were "over 6,000 monasteries and nunneries that served as Tibet's educational institutes in addition to lay schools." The new rulers completely destroyed this system. "During the Cultural Revolution, the Marxist-Leninist-Mao Zedong ideology discouraged the use of minority languages and tried to suppress any sense of minority consciousness. From 1966 Tibetan culture, tradition and society were labeled as "backward" and "blind faith" and Tibetan language, literature, arts and history were denigrated or ignored. Sometime in the 1960s, monk and nun teachers as well as qualified lay Tibetan teachers were ordered to leave their teaching jobs."

Education started to improve in the 1980s, but the exiles report discrimination and cruel practices in the new schools. In *The Next Generation*, a group of refugee children explain exactly why they fled through the snow rather than stay in their school at home. "Children who live in an area where there are schools can choose between a Tibetan or Chinese institution. Tibetan schools are mostly set up by the villagers themselves, without receiving subsidies from the authorities. So facilities are poor. Children can follow lessons in Tibetan, but the problem is that this education doesn't get you much further than primary school. It's almost impossible to find a secondary school in Tibetan. Most Tibetan scholars go through the Chinese system, and start studying their own language as a subject in university."

If you really want to get ahead, you'll have to go to a Chinese institution. It will give you a better chance to be able to attend secondary education in a Chinese province and a university degree. Many children do follow this path. It's not easy, because the Chinese school system is very competitive. Privileged children in Chinese cities already struggle to be the best, since only then will you have a chance to get into a crowded university. Tibetan children struggle from the beginning, much in the same way as other minorities and youngsters from the Chinese countryside do. The children of Chinese cadres also attend the schools and the Tibetan children in

India tell stories of blatant discrimination on every level. "My primary school was a Chinese government school. The school had 200 Tibetan students and 37 teachers of whom 22 were Chinese. I received lessons in Tibetan, math and Chinese. The main teaching language in school was Chinese. I did not understand the Chinese language well enough so I had to ask the teacher again and again. If most of the Tibetans did not understand his explanation in Chinese he used to scold us, calling us 'dirty Tibetans' or 'stupid Tibetans' because we did not understand Chinese," one child is quoted in *The Next Generation*.

As a special thanks to the 'sacrifice' of the parents, Chinese children are said to be given more support in the system. They don't pay tuition and don't need to bribe the teachers to get admitted. "If a Chinese student broke a chair or a book, the government would pay for the new chair or book. If we Tibetans broke anything we had to pay for it ourselves," one child complains. Another adds, "If there was a broken window, or a new class broom was needed, the teachers collected money from the Tibetan students to pay for this. The Chinese students never had to pay anything."

Finally there are the harsh punishments. "When we did not do our homework properly we were kicked and beaten with chairs. Most of the time the teacher hit us on the stomach or the back but sometimes he hit us also on the head. This was the most dangerous because often the wounds had to be stitched. Some students fainted and some had to vomit after these beatings."

Those Tibetans who do get through the educational system, and most of the Tibetans that I met in China had done so successfully, end up going to college. They become veterinarians, doctors or teachers, the kind of professionals that Tibet needs the most. But don't underestimate the strength of the people who get that far. Becoming a teacher, for instance, at the University of Lhasa, means studying in one of the most strictly controlled institutes of China.

I was shown around by a friendly Tibetan educator of the Department of Tibetan Languages. He didn't talk about control, just about subsidies that he receives from the government to buy important Buddhist scriptures. According to *The Next Generation*, this is the only part of the university where lectures are held in the Tibetan language. And this while 80 percent of the students and most educators are Tibetan. History books for the Department of Tibetan History are translated from Chinese. They would have to be; if not, they wouldn't state that Tibet is a historical part of China.

Teachers who want to work at this university are not allowed to be religious, and they have to teach the students the right political ideas. To refuse to do this would be seen as a form of protest and a very bad career move. This way, the teachers keep going back and forth between the urge to educate the people and their own conscience. By adhering to Chinese rules they can instruct the Buddhist texts and keep the language alive. If everything stays quiet, which means that no one protests, they might even be able to set up exchanges with foreign universities. None of this is ideal, the Tibetan scientists who work in Tibet know. But India is far away and not for everyone, and a school under tight control is always better than no school.

ZHAXI CIDAN, UNIVERSITY PROFESSOR IN LHASA

The young professor sits in his office, surrounded by tables and shelves stacked with old Buddhist scriptures. Zhaxi has a young and open face. "These documents here cost 10,000 yuan," he says and points to some scrolls on the table. "We bought them from a monastery. They're expensive, because the monks have to copy them down by hand and that takes a lot of time. The government has given us 150,000 yuan to buy these kinds of manuscripts."

After our interview, Zhaxi shows me the rest of the university. It consists of a few bare, typical Chinese-style buildings. In the computer lab students can send e-mail and use the Internet. "But how do you protect the students against dangerous content?" I ask innocently. The supervisor in the room explains that the computers have special software which records everything the students download.

Zhaxi also introduces me to the head of the Chinese department, another welcoming Chinese man who sacrifices his life to educate the Tibetans. Outside, in front of the entrance, is the usual blackboard. It tells students in Chinese and Tibetan script about the latest campaign of the Communist Party and the decisions taken during the Party Congress. The propaganda is decorated with little, colorful flowers.

"I work for the Department of Tibetan Languages. We have three teachers here. Students learn history; read Buddhist texts and Tibetan language. Sometimes the texts are so old that they're written on stone tablets. We have 1,600 students now at this university. Eighty percent end up being sent out as teachers. There are other departments, like the ones for Chinese and English language and technology. In the Art Department there's traditional dancing, music, tangka drawing and Chinese and Western painting. Then there is math, IT and electronics. I graduated from this university myself. Most of the educators who work here are graduates. This institution was founded in 1956. In the beginning it was only for *ganbus* who came to study Tibetan. In 1976 we became a teacher college and in 1985 a university.

"I'm originally from Lhasa. My father was a tailor; he worked for the monasteries. He was independent, like an entrepreneur. I was born in 1963. My father knew how to read and write, some of his family members had taught him. My mother was illiterate. When I was nine years old, I went to school for the first time. We were all put together in one class. The eldest was 11 and he was also a beginner. This was during the Cultural Revolution and it was all very chaotic. In primary school we had three subjects: Tibetan, Chinese and math. For the first five years, we didn't learn much. We often went on field trips and we wrote *dazhibao*, posters. What did we write about? No idea. I don't remember anything of those texts.

"Secondary school was better, we seriously started to study ten subjects. In the end, I was the best student in the class. Our class was the first one that had to pass an entrance exam to university. The class before us had just gone on. As long as they had the right family background, they could go. But we had to have good grades, and they also looked at which kind of family you were from. I was a little worried, because my parents also possessed some land. But luckily my father's profession was never held against me.

"After my studies I was sent to Beijing. I worked in the Museum for Ethnic Minorities. There were all kinds of exhibitions about the minority cultures. I worked in the library and wasn't very busy; there were very few visitors. Just a few students once in a while who came from a minority background and who were writing a thesis.

"I was in Beijing when the Panchen Lama died. I didn't know him personally. He was an important religious leader, so you couldn't just go and see him. He wasn't in Beijing when he died, but there was a ceremony in the Great Hall of the People to honor him. We all went there, 800 of us. The party leaders also attended. We all bowed to the Panchen's picture and cried.

"It's hard to get used to life in Beijing when you're from Lhasa. There were seven of us who were sent to the capital, and we all ended up coming back here. Most of the Tibetans in Beijing come from Qinghai. For them the climate is not so different. But we are used to the mountains. We can work better here. I also prefer the atmosphere here. Here we are with other Tibetans, and with our Chinese comrades, of course. In the library in Beijing I didn't feel that I was doing anything useful. Here I teach the children, that's more constructive.

"I like being a teacher. Doctors and teachers are among the most respected professions in Tibet. I think I'll always work here. The facilities of the school are not that good yet, but we're working hard to improve. The buildings are a little old. One important thing is that nowadays we have exchanges with foreign universities. There are students who go to Norway for two years, and others go to the United States. I wouldn't mind going abroad for further training myself, but our department didn't set up an exchange program yet. It's mostly the people from the English and IT programs who go.

"In the United States and in Japan there are excellent departments for Tibetan language and culture. Maybe we'll find a way to work with them. In India it's difficult. People there are Buddhist, but they didn't develop the religion as an academic subject. That's what we're trying to do here; we're looking for the scientific approach. We are, after all, a university. When I was small, I was Buddhist. That is our tradition, I was raised that way. But nowadays, I don't practice religion. I go to the temples and read the documents only when I need to do that for my work.

"I didn't know that there was a problem with the Dalai Lama until I was in secondary school. That was in the eighties. The Dalai Lama sent a mission, led by his brother. They came to visit our institute. We had a very nice school and foreigners often came to take a look. That's how I understood that there were Tibetans living abroad. At university we learned about the whole political situation, the actions of the Dalai Lama and the separatists. Here, we follow Mr Redi. He says that the Tibetans in Lhasa, who help with education and development, are the true nationalists.

"We don't have political problems in this school. In 1987 there was a student who participated in the demonstrations and he was expelled and arrested. But now everything is stable. We hope it stays that way."

TENZIN, A STUDENT AT THE TIBETAN CHILDREN'S VILLAGE SCHOOL

On Karma's desk lies a German picture book with somber black-and-white pictures of Tibetan children. They have walked over the mountains and doctors in Katmandu are treating their frozen limbs. The Tibetan children in exile are one of the most dramatic consequences of the conflict in Tibet. Parents give their children to strangers just so they can go to school. The school for orphans, as the children are called, is located behind one of the mountains. When we visit, the students are on holiday, so it's very quiet. Karma shows me a muddy pond in front of the building, which is named after a famous Tibetan lake. A sign says that the children have to learn to keep the water clean and respect nature. This way, when they go back to Tibet, they'll treat the real lake the same way.

An elderly couple who work as host parents in the school give us a ten-year-old girl to interview. She walks on tiny plastic slippers and looks as if we're taking her to the gallows. We buy her a coke and candies. She likes that, but she still looks at us with utter distrust. We sit down on a wall next to the soccer field and Karma tries to make her feel better by talking to her in soft, kind tones. In almost incomprehensible mumbles she tells us that she doesn't know her father, and can vaguely remember her mother. Her mother brought her here herself when she was three years old. "Maybe she'll feel better if we interview her in the presence of the host parents," I suggest, and so we take her back home. But before we reach the friendly couple, the girl runs off. The guardians laugh, shake their heads and show us to another foster child, Tenzin. This girl sits in a dormitory filled with iron bunk beds and tells her story without much emotion. There's no reason to be dramatic, she says, because coming here means the chance of a lifetime.

"In Tibet I never went to school. In our district there wasn't really one. The Chinese school was about a day's travel away, but my parents didn't want to send me there. They said, "If you go there, you'll become

Chinese." Then there was a Tibetan school, three hours by horseback from our house. But nobody told me to go there. I don't know why not, they just never talked about it. I lived in the countryside and took care of the yaks. There was a lot of work to be done. I'm from Kham, my mother still lives there, but my father has died. They were farmers and had some land.

"Both of my parents were illiterate, but later on I went to live with family members in the city and they taught me to read and write a little. I went to them when I was nine. My brother came to get me. We traveled to Lhasa in the back of a truck. Of course my parents let me go. In Kham there was nothing for me, no school, no future. We hoped that I would be able to go to school in Lhasa, but when I arrived, it turned out that I couldn't be admitted anywhere. I didn't have permission to live in Lhasa. So I lived with my family for three years, without studying. I just helped them with the cleaning and the cooking. Then they told me that I should go to India, as there I would be able to study. My family are merchants, so they earned some money. My brother sells clothes. He's very religious and he wanted to go on a pilgrimage to India to see His Holiness, so he took me along.

"We bought permission to travel to the Nepalese border and from there we paid a guide to take us to the other side. At the border, we had to hide for a few days. We tried to cross at night-time, but that wasn't easy. It was scary, because there were Chinese patrols everywhere who kept sending the Tibetans back. We tried to ride in a jeep with people who had passports, but when we got to the border, the custom officials checked every single person. Those who had a passport could go on, and the five of us who didn't were sent back. So we walked for about ten kilometers in the opposite direction and then took a small path into the mountains. Unfortunately, the border patrol had been following us through their binoculars. The jeep was waiting for us on the other side of the border and the Chinese could see exactly what we were planning to do. They yelled at us to come back. They went to the jeep and confiscated the passports of the others. There were two elderly people and the policemen started to beat them. So the other three with us had to go back to the car. Only my brother and I managed to fall behind the group. We hid close to another road. When everybody had gone, we started walking. We walked the whole night. In the end we reached another road and another jeep with Tibetans took us to the first Nepalese city.

"So that's how we came here. My brother did his pilgrimage and went back. He has his business in Tibet, why would he stay here? It's not easy to get a license to do business, only my brother and uncle have one. So they use it to feed the whole family.

"In the beginning I was homesick, but that has gotten better now. I'm 16 and I started in the "Opportunity Class." That's a special class for children who have just arrived. From there on they sent me to secondary school. I'll finish when I'm 19 and then I'll do two years of high school. In the end I hope to start university when I'm 21. I would like to study management at an Indian university. After that I want to work in the Tibetan community here. There's a carpet factory here and many shops. They can all use people who know how to do business. I don't want to go back to Tibet, except of course if it becomes independent.

"If I had stayed in Kham, I would have been married by now. When I left, my mother told me, "Come back as soon as you can, so we can find you a husband." Most of my friends already have children. They don't have a one-child policy in the countryside, there's nobody to check how many children you have. My mother would have found me a husband. In Kham men have a higher status than women. The women do all the work and take care of the kids. Money is not important. If my mother had found a husband, she would have looked at his character, his behavior, and his reputation in the region would have counted. She would have looked for a friendly man who would have treated me well. In Lhasa men and women were already a lot more equal.

"Here I can make up my own mind about whom I want to marry, as long as it's a Tibetan. Our teachers tell us this clearly. It's important that we stay among Tibetans so we can keep our culture and traditions alive. If you go with an Indian man, the community wouldn't accept you any more. I heard about a Tibetan woman who married an Indian man and she was cast out. The same rule applies to Westerners. My family would be very upset if I were to marry a Western man. In any case, now that I'm here, I don't even think about marrying. I'm here to study. That's the most useful thing for me to do right now."

6.

Nowhere as beautiful as home

After three visits to his hometown, Tuomei Namca, a former follower of the Dalai Lama, finally decided to return and settle down in his native Tibet. "Homeland is better than elsewhere after all," he said. Tuomei, 42, who returned to Nyainrong County, Nagqu Prefecture, five years ago, is now a standing member of the Nagqu Prefectural Committee of the Chinese People's Political Consultative Conference.

In the early 1960s, Tuomei left his homeland for India with his father. "Immediately after my graduation from a school for adults in New Delhi, India, I became involved in politics," he says. He followed others in the pursuit of 'independent Tibet,' he said. "I was quite active at the time. Later I became so important that I was assigned to head an agency of the 'Tibetan government-in-exile' in Nepal," he said.

On each March 10 on the traditional Tibetan calendar, senior leaders of the 'government-in-exile' would gather in India for meetings, as the day is considered 'Tibet uprising day' by those Tibetans. "I attended nearly all the meetings in those years, taking part in discussions on how to bring about an 'independent Tibet.' But I gradually grew weary of the activities as time elapsed," he said. "Even though we had initiated many political activities outside China, no country recognizes Tibet as an independent country."

In 1979, the government of the Tibet Autonomous Region announced that it welcomed overseas Tibetans to visit their relatives and friends in China, go sightseeing or settle down in their motherland, with all their misdeeds abroad forgiven. "I half-believed and half-doubted what I had heard on the radio," he said. "But I missed my hometown so much that not long after I set foot in Tibet, I was overcome with mixed feelings."

It so happened that when he returned to his native Nyainrong County, local residents were facing severe hardships because of natural calamities and the central government was sending lots of relief goods and materials to help them. Hard as their life was, the local people did not blame the government, he said. "This made me more confused," Tuomei said. "After a short stay, I left Tibet again."

In 1983, Tuomei returned to Tibet for a second time. During his second stay, he visited local residents from door to door. Later, he went to pastoral areas to visit herdsmen. He also toured Beijing and Shanghai to see changes in the rest of the country. "Seeing is believing," he said. "The party's policies are good. Tibetans have not only enough to eat and wear but also have TV sets to watch. Great changes have taken place throughout China, including Tibet."

In the summer of 1985, Tuomei Namca decided to come back to Tibet together with his wife and four children and not to leave again. Not long after his return, the family was given an apartment. In addition, the local government provided him with a piece of land in a downtown street so his wife could start a business. Soon Tuomei Namca was elected a standing committee member of the CPPCC Nagqu Prefectural Committee. The position carries a monthly salary of 300 yuan.

From late 1989 to early 1990, Nagqu Prefecture was struck by the heaviest blizzard in a century. Tuomei volunteered to take part in relief work. He was appointed to lead a group to help victims rebuild homes and restore production. Heavy snow continued for nearly half a year and reached 150 centimeters in depth. The very existence of the local herdsmen was in danger. Tuomei was at a loss for what to do. A few days later, the central government sent helicopters to ship large quantities of relief goods and materials to the region, including food, medicine and woolen blankets. The supplies ensured basic life necessities for the local people. "Though the calamity lasted for a half a year, no one froze or starved to death," he said. "This was nothing short of a miracle."

That may explain why this former follower of the Dalai Lama is a loyal Chinese without a tittle of regret about his return.
(From *Profiles of 50 Tibetans*, Xinhua Publishing House, Beijing)

I am a Tibetan who was educated in India as a youngster but who returned to Tibet. I worked for various companies in Tibet, and visited different countries in the West. Tibetans inside Tibet can be quite successful in setting up businesses and finding jobs. This is important because we have to take part in the new economy and in all walks of life, and we have to make ourselves less dependent on the Chinese.

This year our businesses were of course hit hard, as we were affected in all spheres of life by everything that happened since March. The situation inside Tibet is desperate. Even in an anonymous letter I am afraid to fully speak out. The names of friends that are in prison can't be mentioned because while they are not yet sentenced, any evidence of a link with the outside world will further jeopardize their situation. Even though things have normalized a little since the end of the Olympic Games, the Chinese authorities use all efforts to silence people inside Tibet and also to create distrust and antagonism between the nationalities. Because of the terrible propaganda on TV *and in other media, Chinese people these days are either afraid of or angry with any Tibetan they meet, while we are left furious when we see the propaganda that is being broadcast on television.*

(From Phayul.com, website of the Tibetan government-in-exile, November 15, 2008)

Stories in the Chinese media make readers believe that Tibetan exiles who want to return to their home country will be welcomed with open arms. But the exiles in India and those who have returned to Tibet tell very different stories. It seems that successful repatriates like Tuomei are few and far between. In Lhasa I asked to interview a returned exile, and even though the Tibetan Bureau for Foreign Affairs did everything to accommodate me, they couldn't find one. And you would expect them to have a model converted refugee readily available for Western journalists. The excuse they had was that the lost sons tend to move back to the countryside, to the places where they're from.

Maybe there's another reason. The Chinese government states that all exiles are welcome, but in practice it doesn't really want them to come back *en masse*. A large number of returnees would be a threat to the authorities. The Chinese can't use too many people who were exposed to the Western press for years, who at one point were followers of the Dalai Lama and were involved in anti-Chinese activities. On the other hand, they do encourage parents whose children have disappeared to India to get them back. Those parents can easily obtain a passport and travel permission.

So the authorities take in a few people, just enough to prove that they mean what they said. These runaways get a house and a salary and in exchange they declare in public that the Dalai Lama is on the wrong path and that the Chinese way is the only one. The propaganda is supposed to discourage others from fleeing, but sometimes it works out the wrong way. A Tibetan told me that the official media once published a book about a refugee who told a long story of suffering and starvation in India. But instead of discouraging flight, Tibetans read it as proof that the Chinese had made them suffer so much, that people had to live through these hardships in India. Soon the book was taken out of the shops.

Those who have been in India expect lots of trouble going back. There are stories of returned exiles put in jail. Even young students, like the boy in the next story, are scared to be captured. Their fear is based on vague stories of "a friend of a friend" who was arrested too. The exiles in India have tried to go back to their homeland in all kinds of ways. Some spend years waiting for official permission for a visit. If they get it, they find a well prepared and heavily controlled hometown. Others want to march back into Tibet in groups of a hundred people. But when a group of Tibetans tried to do this some years ago, the Indian police stopped them. To go by yourself, in secret, is dangerous, most Tibetans in exile agree. Once inside, you'll live on the fringe of society. You won't be able to show your diplomas from India, because you'll be found out, and you won't belong to any work unit. That leaves going back to school or selling goods on the street as the only possibilities. So it's not surprising that most of the refugees stay where they are, in India, even if they're homesick.

The longer the situation in Tibet lasts, the fewer people try to go back. Most of the young people who live in Dharamsala have never been to Tibet. They are fighting for independence for a country that they have never seen. If they ever succeed, they will be in for quite a shock. By now, they have no idea what they wish for.

KAGYA, THE RETURNED EXILE

I meet Kagya (not his real name), a young undergraduate with a wide smile at a university in the Chinese province where he shares a room with five Chinese students. Kagya keeps his study in India a well kept secret. He is less mysterious about his plans for the future. "The last thing I want to do is stay here in the Chinese province. It's too polluted and overpopulated," he says. "I miss the Tibetan climate. I want to go back and help Tibet's development. The Chinese don't do that much. They don't really want the Tibetans to learn much and to develop, because then they'll know many things and become dangerous. The Chinese cadres in Lhasa use most of the money to build tall buildings. Then they say, "Look! Development!" but the Tibetans just stay poor. The Chinese also publish books to show that they're helping education, but nothing structural happens. Tibetans who try to set up projects from abroad don't get permission."

"I'm from North Tibet, my parents were poor farmers. They wanted something better for me, because I'm the eldest son. But I wasn't a very good student, I was quite lazy. My uncle, who lived in Lhasa, heard this and he sent for me. He asked me all kinds of questions, like 'What do you want to be? A truck driver? Or do you want to go to university?' I wasn't even 15 years old. My uncle could help me, so he sent me to India. It cost a thousand yuan for a businessman to take us over to the other side. We were totally dependent on him, and I really respect him because he took a big risk. One thousand yuan isn't a lot of money and I heard stories of smugglers who got caught. They were surrounded by a group of soldiers and those guys just played with them. They used their captives for target practice and kicked and beat them as much as they liked.

"We spent one month walking through the mountains. At night we walked and during the day we hid in the forest. There were many army camps. At that time I knew nothing about Tibet or the situation, I only knew that it was illegal to cross the border like this. But it was impossible to get a passport or permission to travel normally. I still don't have a passport, never had one, only an identity card. I didn't think it was strange that there were so many army camps. My parents had never told me anything. My mother never went to school and my father wasn't home very often. Plus we lived in the North, far away from the capital. Many things happen in the capital that people in the provinces know nothing about.

"The trip was very hard. There were 40 of us and I was the youngest. Soon we ran out of food. We had just a little bit of *tsampa* left. But to eat that, you had to mix it with tea and we couldn't boil water. If we could find wood, we would boil water from snow. Sometimes we used other items, like shoes, to make a fire. Nobody in our group died of starvation or exposure, but I know that sometimes this does happen.

"Once in Nepal, we didn't feel safe either. The Nepalese police like money, so they sometimes arrest Tibetan refugees and rob them; they even take their clothes. Then they give them back to the border police. The Chinese pay them for that. The climate in Nepal was another problem; the heat was terrible. It was as if the earth itself radiated heat. And the parasites! They would stick to your skin and drink your blood. We put special herbs in our shoes to protect ourselves against all those pests.

"Luckily no one discovered us. We made it to the Tibetan Reception Center; there you are safe. The Nepalese police can't get to you and you get food and pocket money. After a while I was taken to Dharamsala. It wasn't as hot there and there were many Tibetans, but I missed my family and my country. I wanted to go on audience with the Dalai Lama, but he was traveling. So I enrolled in school and was put with a group of children my age. They sent me to a place that was seven hours' travel from New Delhi.

"At school I learned about the history of Tibet. We studied culture, language, life of the Dalai Lama and everything the Chinese had done to us. I learned to hate the Chinese. Everything was free at school, even the pens. We also had a foster mother and father who looked after us. The school got funds from people in the West. I also had an American godmother who sent me money. Sometimes she wired more than I needed, so that the rest of the money could be given to other students.

My parents in Tibet were very proud of me, because they heard that I had become the top of the class.

"But after a few years I became sick, I had a kind of chickenpox and I had stomach problems. The doctor treated me for half a year, but after all that time I still wasn't cured. The doctor said that maybe it was the climate and that I couldn't stand the low altitude. So I decided to go back home. I first went to stay with friends in Nepal. There I went to the doctor again, but he also couldn't help me. My friend arranged a car with a driver for me, while my uncle on the other side thought of a way to smuggle me back in.

"You can't just go back into Tibet. I heard that if I got caught, I risked three months in prison. I would be mistreated and have to endure political sessions. The Chinese authorities know that we are dangerous, because we know the truth. They are afraid we'll influence others. I also didn't want to go back the legal way. I know a man who did that. He got a house, but he also had to say bad things about the Dalai Lama on TV. I didn't want to do that; it has a bad influence on the Tibetan people. Of course some would know that you're talking nonsense, but those in faraway provinces might believe what you say.

"Once in Lhasa I wanted to study at the university, but I heard from ex-students that they are very strict there. There is a department of Tibetan language. The schoolbooks are in Tibetan, but translated from Chinese. The history of Tibet is all changed. Plus, you get political lessons during which the teachers try to find out what you think. Almost every week they'll give you a multiple-choice question like who is your leader – A. Deng Xiaoping; B. Dalai Lama; or C. Don't know. My friends always chose "Don't know."

"Luckily I got permission to study at a Chinese university here. I have to pay for myself and I'll never be able to say that I went to India. The Chinese are nicer here and the atmosphere is not so tense. They are different from the Chinese in Lhasa. The Tibetan students here dare to talk about Tibet with Chinese roommates without any problems. I don't hate these Chinese students either. They don't know anything about our problems. If I would refuse the Chinese school system, I would be the one to lose out. Without the system, you can't study and then you can't help your country. I don't talk about politics. If someone starts to talk about it, I tell him that I don't know anything about politics, but that I can explain Tibetan culture if he likes. There are many Tibetan students who say this.

"It's better if the Dalai Lama doesn't come back. Now he is working for Tibet's independence, and he can only do this abroad. Here he would be put away in a monastery somewhere. It could even be dangerous, as some people believe that the Panchen Lama was poisoned. That could happen to the Dalai Lama too. And look how the Chinese handled the reincarnation of the Panchen Lama. What if they do the same thing after the Dalai Lama dies on Tibetan territory?

"I think that the situation in Tibet won't change until China changes. As soon as they become more liberal and democratic, maybe we can find a solution. And until that time, all those who can stand to be in India should stay there, because their work is very important."

7.

MEMBERS OF ONE FAMILY

I always speak very rudely. But it is only for the good of the nation. I have nothing to gain personally from it. Personally, I am quite happy. I feel that I am the happiest man in China. Therefore, you should think in broad terms. What are we gaining from the leftist practices in Tibet? Those with leftist ideology are suppressing everything. When Comrade Hu Yaobang was disgraced recently, the leftist officials exploded firecrackers and drank in celebration. They commented that the stalwart supporter of the Tibetan people had been defeated. They also said that Wu Jinhua, Panchen and Ngabo would not be able to return to Tibet. Why can't we be allowed to return to our homeland? But, as it turned out, they celebrated a bit too early. These are the people who are trying to drive a wedge between the Tibetans and the Chinese. We are members of one family. How dared they say that the Tibetan supporter had been defeated?

The expense of keeping one Chinese in Tibet is equal to that of keeping four in China. Why should Tibet spend its money to feed them? Instead, we should think carefully on how best the money can be used for the development of Tibet. Tibet has suffered greatly because of the policy of sending a large number of useless migrants. The Chinese population in Tibet started with a few thousand and today it has multiplied manifold. That is the reason why many old Chinese personnel who worked very hard in the initial period are left without any career now. Today, the Chinese personnel come to Tibet accompanied by their families. They are like the American mercenaries. They fight and die for money. This is ridiculous.

(Panchen Lama, People's Congress, 1987)

The Chinese girl and her neighbors are all from Sichuan province. Together with her husband she came here, to a deserted street outside of Lhasa that leads into the mountains, to start a restaurant. The situation in her province must have been really hopeless, because it's hard to imagine that this is an improvement. The food stalls are located in a row of brick cubicles that are open on the front. Inside there are three wooden tables and some benches. A black-and-white TV squeaks from a hole in the wall. A bigger opening leads to a kitchen darkened by smoke and filth. "You'd better make sure that the food is good and clean," my translator warns her. "If this foreigner becomes ill, you're going to be in trouble." The girl immediately starts to wipe the benches with a piece of toilet paper.

Competition in this remote place is fierce. As soon as a car stops, and that happens a few times a day, the girls run outside to coax the clients to their places. We soon become the object of a vicious fight. The girl next door had already convinced the translator that we would eat there, but then our current host said something to make her change her mind. The neighbor is now complaining loudly. It's not fair, she yells, as our car is parked in front of her restaurant. She sits in front of her stall on a wooden stool and insults the competition in a heavy provincial accent.

But she doesn't impress the winner at all. "She can't do anything to me," our host proudly announces. "My brother works right over there, in the back. He has a good position in the army. So nobody scares me." A Tibetan man who until now had been noisily slurping his noodles looks up. "What?" he exclaims, "Your brother works in the army? If I had known that, I wouldn't have come here to eat."

These squabbling stallkeepers have no idea that they are the subject of many international discussions. The exiles accuse the Chinese authorities of trying to move as many Chinese to Tibet as they can. That way, Tibet will really become an inseparable part of China.

How many Chinese there are in Tibet is hard to say. Estimates abroad suggest that the Tibetans have become a minority in their own country, and the Chinese outnumber them three to one; others even suggest that the number is six to one. The exiles see each new project, like the recent opening of a super-fast railway line, as a plot to get more Chinese into the region.

Although this high ratio of Chinese might be possible in the lower parts of Tibet that border Chinese provinces, it's certainly not true in Lhasa. While the economy there is clearly in the hands of the Chinese – they own the shops and restaurants – the majority of people on the street are Tibetans. But the Tibetans, who for centuries didn't let in any foreigners at all, feel overwhelmed by the Chinese presence anyway.

Every time the Chinese government is accused of an immigration policy, they point out that it is impossible to get many Chinese to live in the region. Wu Yingjie, a top publicity official of the regional government, made the comments recently in response to a question by a foreign journalist over whether immigrants would flood in and destroy the plateau's ecology with the launch of the railway. "Tibet's unique natural conditions make it impossible for Han people, and people from other ethnic groups, to settle down here," said Wu. For the Chinese, the whole discussion is nonsense anyway as, according to theory, Tibet and China belong to the same country. "The Tibetans and the other 55 Chinese ethnic groups are members of one big family," Wu explained once again. "It's natural for them to conduct exchanges freely." But when pressed for figures, the politician stated that "Today, Tibet's population has expanded to 2.7 million, with Tibetans accounting for 95 percent."

Chinese media often report how soldiers and cadres have to be promised extra bonuses or have to be forced to go, and the businesspeople and workers only want to be there in summertime. Chinese media like to boast about the great provisions that cadres get when working in Tibet. One article describes how the army leaders spent 150,000 yuan to buy 15 TV sets and the construction of a school for the soldiers and their children so as to 'soften their worries and troubles.' The children who are taken along to Tibet can study for free, and the entry exams to university are not as difficult as in the rest of China.

Despite the perks, many cadres see a transfer to Tibet as a demotion and some even refuse to go. This was the case of a vice mayor of a town in eastern China. The man was responsible for the development of industry in his region until his bosses decided, after some medical tests, that he would do a great job in Tibet. He refused and as a punishment was fired from the local standing party committee. His refusal came at a bad time, as there was a campaign going on to honor the people's hero Kong Fan Sen. This man had been a Chinese cadre, had dedicated his life to the development of Tibet and had died doing so.

You can see that it's difficult for the Chinese to live in Lhasa. It starts with the high altitude. The Chinese seem to have big trouble adjusting and often get sick. Chinese men generally do not have very healthy lifestyles. Smoking and drinking is part of the male identity and exercise is for schoolchildren. The worse shape they are in, the harder it is to breathe in the thin mountain air. Breathing problems are fast followed by stabbing headaches and nausea.

There are personal problems too. One woman tells me that very few Tibetan women marry Chinese men now, but that this happened a lot in the 1960s. Not only was it politically correct at that time, it was also an easy way to a better life. But the woman says that many of those marriages now break up. After many years of working in Tibet, the husband wants to retire to China, but the Tibetan woman refuses to go with him.

You see many unhappy Chinese in Tibet. At my hotel, for instance, the former Holiday Inn, guests have breakfast in the Hard Yak Café. A beautifully made-up Chinese woman is the host. She looks as if she just walked out of a Hollywood movie from the sixties. The Tibetans serve food. They have a talent for this kind of job, as they are friendly and smile easily. The Chinese boss, on the other hand, puts on a stern face that doesn't match her appearance. She seems irritated that she can't understand her staff. "What are you two talking about?" she yells at them one morning while I'm having breakfast. "Stop talking and work!"

Tibet is poor, strange and barbaric to the Chinese, and to make matters worse, it's also a scary place. The cadres are told that they have to watch out for the enemy. Every Tibetan is a potential troublemaker or a spy, encouraged by the Dalai Lama to carry out terrorist activities. The Chinese are so paranoid that sometimes the army suddenly gets mobilized because of a rumor that the Dalai Lama is staging another campaign.

But there is improvement also in the negative image that the Chinese have of the Tibetans. Inside China, people are becoming interested in the colorful Tibetan culture. Writers and musicians let themselves be inspired by it. The Chinese media encourage this. Daily, people can watch the beauty of Tibetan religious ceremonies on TV. Another helpful influence is that Buddhism is becoming popular in China itself, which brings more interest in the Tibetan lamas and monasteries. The Chinese man who works for the Tibet Bureau in Chengdu, a department of the Foreign Ministry that takes care that all official diplomats and journalists take the right plane to Lhasa, is also a Buddhist. He speaks English fluently, and was an active and good student at the university, but instead of dreaming about studies in America, he talks about Tibet. In Chengdu, he tells me, he regularly visits the local Tibetan temples and listens to lectures about

Buddhism by the Tibetan lamas. "I wouldn't mind working in Lhasa for a while," he says. "I don't understand why others don't want to."

The Dalai Lama, meanwhile, tries to convince his followers that Chinese people are humans too. Persuading his followers that cruel monsters do not occupy Tibet is not easy, especially to people who were jailed or tortured. By now, several generations of Tibetans have grown up in exile. They never knew the Chinese but have been taught to hate them. And Western pro-Tibet activists often don't believe in nuance either.

The religious leader, however, likes to say that he admired Mao Zedong. In his autobiography he writes about meeting the Chinese leader for the first time.

"As we entered the hall, the first thing I noticed was an array of spotlights that had been erected for a whole army of official photographers. Beneath these stood Mao himself, looking very calm and relaxed. He did not have the aura of a particularly intelligent man. However, as we shook hands, I felt as if I was in the presence of a strong magnetic force. He came across as being very friendly and spontaneous, despite the formality of the occasion. ... Every time I saw Mao, he inspired me again."

He had the same favorable impression of the Chinese people themselves. "I could see that a lot of people had given up everything in order to help bring about a transformation in society. Many bore physical scars from the struggle and most were men of the highest principle who genuinely sought to bring about real benefits for every person in their vast country. ... They were so passionate about their ideals that they would stop at nothing to achieve them."

Tibet's highest lama goes on to admit that he still doesn't understand how these people could come to do such barbaric things. "I remain at a loss to explain how this happened, how the noble ideals of so many good men and women became transformed into senseless barbarity. ... It seems that China is a country which has lost its faith, as a result of which the

Chinese people themselves have endured unspeakable misery over the past 41 years, all in the name of communism," he writes.

The religious leader also describes with wonder how the Chinese seem to believe their own claims. A party leader from Beijing once visited Tibet and asked a woman there what she thought about the Chinese. The woman gave the standard answer, that the Chinese and Tibetans were members of the same family, or something like that. The party leader went home satisfied. He had found proof that the Tibetan people loved the Chinese.

It still works like that. Xiao, the Chinese cadre in the next interview, really does believe that Tibet is part of China and that he is there to help the people. He sees himself as an aid worker and Tibetan demonstrators are, to his way of thinking, criminals out to disturb his life's work. Xiao becomes furious if you try to defend them. He is one of many people who grew up with the Chinese propaganda. It has always told him that he must dismiss all information from the West about Tibet, because those stories are nonsense written by anti-communist Westerners who don't want China to become powerful. He will never find out what the population really thinks of him, because they will never tell him. There are other Chinese people who take care of that.

XIAO HUAI YUAN, THE CHINESE CADRE

"Live your life serving the people" is written in gold characters on the wall of Xiao's office building. On the other side stands a chalkboard. The contributions of the cadres to the snowed-in nomads are registered there. "Look," Xiao says. "My name is there. I donated three hundred yuan, the most of everybody. You tell me, Mrs. An, isn't that the way to help the people?" Xiao has a round, spotty face and yellow teeth. He works in a nice-looking, but stone-cold, office. He finds a package of seeds from

New Zealand in front of his door, products he's planning to try out in the Tibetan countryside.

Xiao is an engineer and he loves to talk about his work. He has taken the afternoon off to tell me all about it. Tibetan products are laid out on the table; bottles of mineral water, glass pots with black and better-looking brown seeds. "Look," Xiao says. "This is what the Tibetans produced before we started helping them." He shows me the pot with black, broken seeds. "And this is what they are eating now." Those are the brown seeds. "You tell me, Mrs. An. What would you prefer? Even the yaks won't eat this black stuff. How can people live off it?"

After listening politely for two hours to a lecture about his projects, I almost have to pull his life story out of him. And then we start a tough discussion about the Chinese in Tibet. He is one of the few people here with whom I can safely have this argument. I'm sure that he believes in what he says.

"Look, here is another product that we developed. It's called Rhodiola, a traditional medicine. If we don't develop the local economy, how will we be able to earn money for education and cultural events? The sale of this product alone got us 6.5 million yuan in income taxes. None of those earnings go to Beijing; it's all used to help develop the region. Mao Zedong said, "Go to Tibet, but don't eat the people's food," and we never did. When we were revolutionaries and lived with the nomads, we paid for our food. In those times, a sheep cost ten yuan and we needed two a month. In the old Tibet, people were hungry, but nowadays they're well fed. Even during the Cultural Revolution people continued to work on the land. There wasn't a lot of food around, but there was enough.

"I'm from Shanxi province, from the countryside. My father and mother worked in the army. My father left for Tibet in 1950; he was one of the first. He was in charge of finances. In 1952 he had to go to Beijing to report on the financial situation in his area and after that he came home, to Lanzhou. I was born a year later. When I was two weeks old, my parents both left for Tibet. They left me with my uncle, in a village close to Lanzhou. So I'm a good farmer, because I lived in the countryside until I was 19 years old. Now I'm 54, and my father never took care of me.

"By the time I became an adult, my parents came back to retire. They had three children and hoped that one of us would continue their work for Tibet. My father had given me a book with beautiful pictures of the mountains. I used to sleep with it under my pillow. My parents were very proud of the work they did. Most Chinese *ganbus* here are happy to be able to help the people. Some don't of course, not everybody likes it here, it's not a rich area and life isn't easy.

"I studied Tibetan and economics at the College for Ethnic Minorities in Shanxi. I came here in 1974. That was during the Cultural Revolution. We, young revolutionaries, went to live with the nomads for a year. Some people went to live with families, but we had our own tent, which I shared with nine others. During the day we helped the nomads with the work and at night we educated them. Most of that group of youngsters is still here in Lhasa. That year left a big impression on me. I saw how poor the population was and how urgently they needed education and development.

"After that I taught at the University of Agriculture and Husbandry in Amdo for eight years. I loved teaching. My former students are all over Tibet; they all became *ganbus*. I also wrote a book. Here, I still have some copies. It's about the history of Tibetan money. When I was in the countryside I noticed that there were no books on this subject. So mine is seen as one of the best works.

"In the nineties I was transferred to Lhasa. Here I became director of the Economic Development Center and head of the Economic Reform Committee. In 1992 we started the reforms of the state industry, since we had more than 400 state factories here. We chose 66 important ones, a tannery, a cement factory, and a few trading companies, and made them the focus of our reforms. Industry is important; we have tried to adjust the system so that the state factories become more efficient and profitable. We now also have companies in Tibet that can trade shares. I was personally involved in approving the first two.

"But I also love science and technology, so now I'm also head of the Science and Technology Committee. Before, there was no science in Tibet and there were no factories. There were only a few traditional workshops. In 1942 they built a power station, but that broke down two years later. The only factory was the one that produced money. The People's Liberation Army built everything you see. When I came here, people had no food. We would go visit friends around dinnertime, so they would feed us. And everywhere the side of the road was one big public toilet.

"But let me tell you more about my work, Mrs. An. It's very difficult to introduce technology in this country. People are too superstitious. If it hails, people start praying. I want to introduce solar panels, but people think that the sun is a spirit. They believe that if we use solar energy, the spirits will get tired. Look at that picture on the wall. That's me with some monks in the province. We also gave them solar heaters, so now they can boil water. I want to introduce as much technology as I can, but it's a very slow process.

"On the other hand, people can't go on like this, having dirty faces, brown teeth and nothing to eat. They need sufficient food and an education. Money is important everywhere in the world and Tibet is no exception. You have to eat first, and then you can be religious. You Westerners think having human rights means the freedom to be Buddhist. You make a lot of noise about a few prisoners. But if the people could choose, they would choose food first. Why would Tibet be different in that than anywhere else in the world?

"I also like to educate the people about popular science. For example, there are many children here who suffer from iodine deficiency. So we published this brochure about food and nutrition. Then we put out a similar book about animal illnesses and another one about protection of plants in the countryside. I also want to write a book about the sun and the moon, explaining why it rains and why there is hail. We also write books about hygiene which tell the people that they should wash, go to see a doctor when they're pregnant, have children in the hospital instead of in a tent. Things are improving. Young people are starting to know these things. In China we have a book called "A Thousand Whys" in which all these kinds of things are explained. I would like to publish something like that here.

"Except for that, we also try to work on environmental issues. We don't want to make the mistakes that you Westerners made, first polluting everything and then having to clean up afterwards. I traveled to Germany for research, and I saw how they keep their surroundings clean. If anyone wants to start a company, they first need permission from the Bureau for Environmental Protection. We also have protected areas like Mount Everest, animal parks and rivers, that we give extra attention, and we take care that we plant more trees than we cut down. By now the local population knows not to kill the plants. We arrest them if they do. They get at least two weeks in prison if they destroy the environment, but we haven't punished anybody in a long time. We also keep up the research into plants and animals in Tibet because there are many unique species.

"What? Nuclear experiments by the Chinese army in Tibet? No, absolutely not. Mrs. An, I can assure you that no nuclear tests have ever been carried out. Of course I know what the army does around here. I have traveled all over Tibet, I've seen all the roads. Do you think that if someone was exploding bombs, I wouldn't have noticed? I've never seen a big hole. Under the ground? What kind of nonsense is that? And they can measure it abroad? All that is propaganda from the West. They are just looking for reasons to attack us. The Westerners are against the Communist Party. Look at Russia. When there was communism, the Westerners had all kinds of complaints; this was not good, that was not good. Now that there is no more Communist Party, you don't hear them any more.

"The West also uses the Dalai Lama. He is a man with two faces. He says that he wants to help the Tibetan people, but he only does bad things. I was in Lhasa in 1987. When people started to demonstrate, I thought immediately, "Their leaders are bad criminals." They had to be punished. Of course there were only a few organizers. Most of the people were followers who didn't know what they were asking. The children were paid five mao for throwing stones. Those naive followers just need to be educated. The demonstrations really upset the daily life of the people. You couldn't go anywhere and shops were closed so the shopkeepers couldn't earn any money. In any case, I have traveled to many countries. I know that every country has these kinds of problems from time to time.

"What I don't understand is how they could give the Nobel Peace Prize to the Dalai Lama. What did that man ever do for peace? He only makes trouble. He doesn't represent the Tibetans any more. The Tibetans aren't a poor ignorant mountain population like they were in the old Tibet. Nowadays they are educated and know about the size of the world. If the Dalai Lama keeps doing what he does now, there will never be a compromise. He needs to give up his claims for independence. He did that? No, that's not true. He says that he doesn't want independence, but he's lying. And he needs to stop letting himself be used by the West. And anyway, how can he come back? We can't go back in time 50 years, take away the cars, let the people walk again and get back the Dalai Lama.

"Do you know, Mrs. An, what a living Buddha is? According to Tibetan religion, a living Buddha is a god who came back to earth to take care of the people. That's exactly what the Communist Party does. The party is the best kind of living Buddha. I do my job here, and I know it's useful. I am one of 30,000 *ganbus* in Tibet. There are also 70,000 Tibetan leaders.

"The future of the Tibetans? Hand me my calculator, will you? Let me count. We started development in 1965. If we keep going the way we are now, then the Tibetan countryside will be developed, people will have enough food, children will all be able to attend secondary school and there will be good medical care and a high cultural level by the year 2015. We should be able to make that. But that can only happen if we keep the Dalai Lama out and if the country stays stable.

"Myself, I don't know how much longer I'll be able to work here. I have started to suffer from high blood pressure. So I think that I'll go back to my region soon. I hope that after my death, someone will write on my gravestone, '26 years in Tibet, son of the Tibetan people'."

DAWA TSERING, THE FORMER CHINESE

"I was so Chinese that I even wanted to change my name. The problem was that no Chinese has 'Da' as a surname. I looked everywhere. Finally I did find a Chinese historical figure who had been called Da. I was so happy! Finally I had adapted completely. When I was 20 years old, I only spoke Chinese. I did speak some Tibetan with my parents, but even then, I would be thinking in Chinese, and then translate that in my head into Tibetan."

Dawa is now a refugee living in Dharamsala. He never interrupts his laugh, even when he relates the story of how he was beaten by Chinese prison guards. He sits next to a desk burdened by heaps of papers. He is the editor of a magazine in Chinese which tries to inform the Chinese people about the real situation in Tibet.

He didn't always believe that giving information was the key to solving the problems of Tibet. "I was in the same prison as Chinese dissident Wei Jingsheng. I knew he was a dissident, but he was also a Han, so I didn't have anything to do with him. I figured that his struggle against the Communist Party wasn't my problem."

"Look, I'll draw you a map. This used to be the Tibetan province of Kham, but the upper part, the North, became the Chinese province of Qinghai. And the eastern part of Kham became Sichuan. That way, our province became smaller and smaller until almost nothing was left. This is where I grew up. My father worked for the Chinese, he transported their goods. I think he didn't like them at all, but he never said that. I think he only worked for them because we had to eat. But he would never admit his real feelings, also to protect me. Sometimes he did talk about the Chinese with his friends, and then I saw hate in his eyes.

"I went to a Chinese school where we only learned Chinese language. It was during the Cultural Revolution and at that time, there were no Tibetan schools. Now there are some, but still not that many. So until I was 20 years old, I was only able to speak a little Tibetan. I couldn't read or write it at all. In those schools, we were educated to become Chinese. We saw how the Chinese arrested and punished people, but whenever we saw that, we were convinced that those accused were bad criminals, so it was normal that they were punished. The father of one of my friends was attacked during a self-criticism session. My friend immediately didn't want to have anything to do with his father. We were also told to ask our fathers about their political ideas, and then report about it at school. But my father never answered my questions. He knew that was too dangerous.

"One day, I came home from school and heard a strange noise in a big old cupboard which my parents had put in our courtyard. I thought that an animal must have gotten inside, and was now locked in. But when I opened the door, I saw my grandmother and my father secretly praying to a big Buddha statue. It gave me such a shock that I ran off. My father chased after me. When he got hold of me, he said, 'If you say one word to your teacher about what you just saw, I will beat the living daylights out of you.' After he had gone, I went to sit next to the river to think. I was wearing my red scarf, a sign that I was a good revolutionary. I didn't know what to do: tell the truth about my father and get beaten up, or stay quiet and risk losing my revolutionary honor if the secret was discovered. In the end I chose for my father, since I was more scared of being beaten.

"When I was small, the Chinese were our heroes, but then I started to grow up and slowly I started to understand that they looked down on us. My Chinese friends called the Tibetans barbarians. They would say that I wasn't a barbarian any more, as I spoke Chinese, and they called that a sign of civilization. They thought themselves very superior to the Tibetans, for no reason, of course. I started to grow away from them and became more interested in my own culture and people. I started to dislike the Chinese, not because I was religious – I wasn't – but because I became aware of the racial tensions between us. I realized I would never be a Chinese. So I asked my parents to tell me about Tibetan traditions and started to learn my own language.

"Meanwhile I had become a police officer. That was another dramatic event in our house. My father wanted me to become a driver, like him. He didn't want me to go to the police academy. I think he was afraid that I would become a bad person. But my grandmother wanted me to get an education. Drivers only get accidents, she said, and as she was older, her word prevailed. They got into a big fight and my grandmother started beating my father. It was strange, because normally my father decides everything for me. He came here a few years ago, saw that I wasn't married, and so he got me a wife. Because of him I'm married now. But that time, my grandmother put her foot down. Nobody asked my opinion, but then they already knew I wanted to be a policeman. I thought it was a real man's job. You got a great-looking uniform and everybody was scared of you.

"One day, when I had been a policeman for three years, we arrested a Chinese man. He had been fighting in the street with a Tibetan guy. During interrogation, he kept talking about 'that *laozhangzhu*' (a way to insult Tibetans). Every time he said that, I got so angry that I slapped him in his face. But he just kept saying it. It was such a habit for him to insult the Tibetans that he had trouble changing his language. I had to slap him many times before he started to talk about 'the Tibetan comrade.'

"When my father heard that I had hit that man, he didn't let me go to work any more. I stayed home for a week, until my boss, who liked me, came to talk to my father. He promised my father that if I ever hit someone again, he would see to it that I would be locked up immediately. So my father let me go back again.

"My boss kept his promise. Some time later, there was another fight in the street. Two Tibetans had driven into a Chinese car. The only thing I did was try to separate them and to do that, I had to pull the Chinese guy by his shirt. But when we came to the bureau, he started complaining that I had hit him. I was locked up for two weeks.

"Around that time, my friends and I started talking about joining the Tibetan freedom fighters. That seemed like paradise, to fight for our country against the Chinese. We had concluded that our lives had no meaning. We worked, but we didn't do anything useful. We wanted to fight like real men. Talking this way, we got ourselves all worked up. Until we got this plan, it seemed that there was nothing we could do. China was so big, there were so many Chinese. But after we thought up our scheme, we felt we had found the way. The first thing we needed were guns, so we broke into the police arsenal. It wasn't our lucky night – there were no guns there at all. We only found bullets, which we took.

"We didn't get far, though. I don't know how the police found out, but we were caught the next day. There were four of us. One of us was jobless and he told us: "Let me say that I'm the leader. It's better they lock me up for a long time. That way you'll get lighter sentences." But when my father heard about this, he became furious. He told me, "You want to be a man, and then you agree to put all the blame on your friend?" So I told the police that I had been the leader and they believed me. I was sentenced to 12 years in prison. In the end I spent only six, as my father never stopped begging for my release.

"They sent me to a prison in Xinning. We had to work every day. The Chinese prisoners had lighter work than the Tibetans. The guards would say, "Those Tibetans are used to looking at the behinds of a bunch of yaks, let them work." They also told the other Tibetan prisoners: "Why do you keep speaking Tibetan? Look at Dawa. He is intelligent. He speaks Chinese well." This really embarrassed me, but I didn't say anything. Back in my cell, I threw away all my Chinese books. The other prisoners lent me their Tibetan books and that's how I learned to read and write my own language.

"Trouble started when I refused to work. In the beginning it wasn't so bad; they let me make furniture. But then they decided that I should carry heavy bags. I couldn't do it; those sacks were too heavy. I thought, I'm going to break my back doing this, so I refused. The guards surrounded me and started beating me with electrical prods and with their fists. They hit and they hit some more and I started bleeding, but I still refused to get up. I figured that if I could get though this torture, they would give me lighter work. In the end I lost consciousness and they threw me into my cell. They were afraid I would die and then they could say that I had just died there. When I woke up, I found I had won. I was put in the place for elderly and handicapped, and you didn't need to work there. But I had to remember to keep walking with a bent back. Sometimes I would forget to limp and the guards would give me work. But it was always light labor.

"I was released after six years. They wanted to send me to work in a place far away from home, but I had already decided to flee to India. I still wanted to join the freedom fighters and I thought that in India they would give me a gun. I had always read the Chinese propaganda which stated that the Dalai Lama staged violent rebellions. That's what I wanted to join, but first I had to help my family. I had to build houses for my father and my sisters. I was the eldest son and I thought that I might die during battle, so I wanted to have them well taken care of. I spent three years building their houses. After I fled, the Chinese came and tore down my father's house. He had to go live outside of town and he lost his job, but my father isn't angry about that. He is old and wants to take care of his health, so he doesn't upset himself.

"When I arrived here, I immediately went to the government-in-exile and asked them for a gun so I could start fighting. They told me that they only work in a peaceful way, and that they didn't have arms. At first, I didn't believe them, but I slowly saw that they were right. Nobody here is trying to organize an armed rebellion. Meanwhile, they have convinced me that they are right. I see many young men arriving here who want to fight, just like I did. I give them a lecture. When they say, "I want to die for Tibet," I answer, "Maybe it doesn't matter to you, but what about your parents?" Then they answer, "Maybe my parents will go crazy if I die."

"Some old friends tell me, "Dawa, how come you have changed so much? Did you forget about Tibet?" Then I answer that I haven't given up the struggle, but that I don't believe in sacrificing myself for nothing. That's why I don't participate in hunger strikes. Those don't put any pressure on the Communist Party. The party leaders do as they please, and they keep the West satisfied by releasing a Wang Dan or a Wei Jingsheng once in a while.

"I have been here now for many years, and by now I am convinced that our only hope is to change the Chinese mentality. That's why we should talk with Chinese dissidents. We produce our magazine here and send as many copies as we can to Chinese people. When I was in jail with Wei Jingsheng, I never thought that talking to him would be useful. But now I see that people are different. Recently we had a Chinese visitor here. When she heard all our stories, she started crying. She said, "As a Chinese, I am also responsible for everything that has been done to you.

I believed that you were political dissidents, but here I can see that you only want peace and the right to practice your religion." And that's the way it is. The Chinese always state that we have to develop, but we can live without cars. Horses are comfortable too, even though we are not against cars either.

"Personally, I think we should all go back together, not one by one. I know a boy who went back to Tibet by himself. We tried to talk him out of it, but he didn't listen. He completely disappeared until someone found him on the streets of Chengdu a year later. He had gone completely mad. Who knows what the Chinese had done to him? I think we should go back in groups, hundreds of people together. They can't make hundreds of people disappear at the same time. We will tear up our Indian passports and walk to the border. But there aren't many refugees who really want that. They claim that the Dalai Lama doesn't want them to do this, even though His Holiness never said that. Much of the work we are doing here, all that talk with Western governments, makes no sense at all. Those foreign governments all want to do business with China. When you go to see them, it's like they're acting out a play. They walk around as if they were kings and queens, they smile nicely, but in fact they could care less about us.

"My father visited me here a few years ago. There was a new law which stated that you could easily get permission to come here if you wanted to go get your child. He came and took my younger brother. I didn't want to go back, so he found me a wife.

"My father wouldn't want to live here. He doesn't know the language, couldn't even find the toilet, that's not a life for him. In Tibet he earns money by trading goods. My father is about the same age as the Dalai Lama. They should both have another ten years to live. That's enough time to be able to see a positive change in Tibet."

8.

THAT MAN CALLED PANCHEN

There was one woman, a wife of one of my staff, who was also arrested. One day, when she was called into the interrogation chamber, she muttered, "This man called Panchen has caused me so much suffering that I will die of depression." This utterance led the authorities into believing that she would say something incriminating about me, a much-awaited chance for the authorities to take punitive measures against me. They immediately called the scribes to record her testimony. Then she went on, "We made a big mistake by following this man called Panchen and not participating in the fight against the Chinese. If he had led us in rebellion against the Chinese, our condition today would be better than this. Because, initially, we would have killed as many Chinese as possible and then fled to India, which would have been easy since India is near our village. But this man told us to be progressive and patriotic. And this is what we get for following his advice. Now it is not possible for us to flee to India. Our people, both men and women, are being persecuted here. We are experiencing hell on earth."

(Panchen Lama, March 1987)

The tenth Panchen Lama, Choekyi Gyaltsen, was a controversial figure who tried to deal with the Chinese in his own way. Widely regarded as a puppet of Beijing at first, he became a hero of his own kind for daring to speak up to the Chinese government while working and living in China.

Being contentious must have come naturally to him. Traditionally, the Panchen Lamas were the teachers of the Dalai Lamas, which gave them the status of the second most important leaders of the country. But there were often problems, as you might expect when there are two great leaders in one religious sect. Throughout the history of Tibet, teacher and pupil were often rivals, with the Panchen Lama ending up as a friend of neighboring China. The emperor of the Qing Dynasty, for instance, nominated a Panchen Lama as the ruler of Tsang and Western Tibet. The Ninth Panchen Lama, who lived from 1883-1937, fled to China after a disagreement with the 13th Dalai Lama about taxes and the autonomy of the Tashilhunpo monastery, the home base of the Panchens. From China, he worked on plans to modernize Tibet. His reincarnation, the famous Panchen Lama of our times, went unrecognized by the former Dalai Lama for years because the Panchen's advisors refused to bring him to Lhasa and submit him to traditional tests. He was enthroned after Chinese officials from the Kuomintang administration approved his selection. Not until he met the current Dalai Lama in 1952 did Tibet's highest authority approve of him.

Maybe it was this relationship with the Chinese during former lives that influenced Choekyi Gyaltsen. The young Panchen became, together with the Dalai Lama, a member of the Preparatory Committee of the Autonomous Region of Tibet. In 1954 the two leaders went to Beijing together to attend the first session of the first National People's Congress. They met Mao Zedong and other leaders. The Panchen Lama also went to India on a pilgrimage with the Dalai Lama, but when the Dalai Lama fled to India in 1959, the Panchen Lama stayed behind.

The outside world soon regarded him as a marionette of the Chinese. After all, he initially supported China's claim of sovereignty over Tibet, and China's reform policies. Even now the Chinese media describe him as a socialist hero: "During his visit to Zhaxi Lhunbo, the ninth-largest Tibetan Buddhism temple in Tibet, Hu (Jintao) dedicated a piece of *hada* (a silk scarf traditionally regarded as a token of respect) to the stupa of the holy body of the Tenth Panchen Lama. Hu praised the contributions of the temple's lamas for the country's unification and unity of all ethnic groups. He encouraged them to pass on the tradition of the Tenth Panchen Lama's patriotism and continue to make new contributions to Tibet's development." (*China Daily*, July 22, 2001).

In Tibet, however, Choekyi Gyaltsen is a very different kind of hero. It turned out that the religious leader who stayed behind spent his life criticizing China's policies in Tibet and trying to modernize his country. It was unknown in the West until 1996 that the Panchen Lama started condemning the Chinese authorities right from the beginning. And because the Chinese wanted him so much as a puppet figure, he had access to the highest leaders. In a document of 70,000 characters which he presented to Premier Zhou Enlai, he explained how disastrous the party's policy was for the Tibetan region. He asked for more environmental protection, more freedom, and more money. He denounced the harsh punishment after the revolts and described how the communes during the Great Leap Forward led to famine.

Zhou at first reacted positively to his petition, but soon afterwards it got the lama into trouble. Instead of changing the policy, Mao Zedong told the Panchen to formally take over the position of the Dalai Lama as highest spiritual leader. Choekyi Gyaltsen refused. In 1964, during the Monlam festival, the 24-year-old Panchen declared to a large crowd of Tibetans that he believed that Tibet would one day become independent again and that the Dalai Lama would return in all his glory.

The result of this speech was a 14-year stay in jail. The Chinese started a "Break the Panchen Lama" campaign. All those who had been close to the leader were interrogated and many were punished as well. The media printed all kinds of accusations; Choekyi Gyaltsen was said to have criticized China unjustly and built up a secret army. The Chinese even accused him of having orgies.

He was freed and reinstated in 1987 and for a few years the Tibetans didn't hear anything anti-Chinese from him. He lived in Beijing, in a small palace next to the Forbidden City. The house became a meeting point for Tibetans living in the capital. The Panchen Lama married a Chinese woman and had a daughter, another controversy. One of my Tibetan friends took me to the small palace one day. It was as if I had stepped into a movie. We were received by a Chinese fairy princess, surrounded by courtiers. We exchanged Chinese gallantries. "You should come more often to play," she said.

But the Panchen Lama hadn't been defeated after all. After his release, he continued to use his ties to the Chinese government to help his country. This looked like a good plan in the 1980s. Hu Yaobang was in charge and he also wanted to repair the damage in Tibet. One of the first things the religious leader did was find promising young people to do the work. Everywhere in China and Tibet you can still meet them, Tibetans who were inspired because the Panchen Lama took them under his wing. The young men set up the Gangjian company, which managed all kinds of projects. They opened factories and shops in an attempt to get the economy back into the hands of Tibetans.

Not long before his death, the Panchen Lama started to speak up again. In 1989 he returned to Tibet for the first time in almost 30 years. There, he delivered his final and now famous speech. "Since liberation, there has certainly been development, but the price paid for this development has been greater than the gains," he concluded. Five days later he died of a sudden heart attack. Rumors have it that the Chinese authorities had had enough and poisoned him, while others believe in a more mystic ending; the Panchen Lama knew he was going to die and went back to his monastery for that purpose.

Most of his plans for Tibet died with him. The Gangjian enterprise prospered while the Panchen Lama was alive, but after his sudden demise, things went downhill fast. The corporation ended up in the hands of the monastery. Many of the promising young recruits didn't want to work for these lamas and they started their own businesses. Nowadays, only a few shops remain and the carpet factory, which is managed by a famous Tibetan businessman, is still running. The man in the next story is one of those who try to keep the dream alive.

To some, the Panchen Lama is more of a hero than the Dalai Lama. "I think the Dalai Lama should come back and do something for the country, just like the Panchen Lama did," a student told me. "The Panchen Lama tried to show that within the system there were ways to improve the situation." Others disagree. They argue that all of the Panchen Lama's accomplishments were in vain and if nothing else, his life shows that there is no room at all for improvement as long as the Chinese are in charge of Tibet.

TSEWANG NYIMA, TIBETAN DEVELOPMENT FUND

The Tibetan Development Fund is housed in a hotel room of the new, luxurious, Tibet Hotel. From his small office, which is a hotel room-turned-workspace, Tsewang tries to help his people by continuing the Panchen Lama's work. Once there was plan to build a beautiful new office complex for the Gangjian Corporation. Tsewang still has the model. But without the stubborn Panchen Lama, the project didn't happen. Tsewang gives me an article in which all his achievements are listed. "There are so many things that need to improve in Tibet. Once I met a dying man. He couldn't speak any more, he only pointed at his two children. I understood that he wanted me to take care of them. I soon discovered that there are many orphans in Tibet. So we built an orphanage."

"My name means "live as long as the sun." The 11th Dalai Lama was from our town, in Eastern Tibet, Doufu County, what is now the province of Sichuan. Our region is not very developed. My parents were farmers and they owned plots of land. I never spent a lot of time with them. There weren't many schools in our district. Primary school was already far and secondary school was 70 kilometers away, so we had to go live with other people fairly early. After that I studied Tibetan languages.

"So there I was when the Panchen Lama came to visit one of the regions next to ours. It was about 200 kilometers away from us. I heard that you could enter an exam and that the best would be chosen to work for the Panchen Lama. I knew that I had to go. What chances would I have if I stayed in the countryside? There weren't many jobs there. So I bought a ticket. I took the bus to Ganzi, where the exams took place.

"The Panchen Lama came with another famous living Buddha, who was from our area. He had escaped to Switzerland, but the Panchen Lama had told him after 30 years to come back home. This way he could help to develop the region. People were delighted with their visit. We were told to wait for three days before we could sit for the exam. The night before the test, I had a dream; the Panchen Lama gave me a traditional Tibetan shawl. When I woke up the next day, I was full of courage. I knew I had a chance.

"But when I arrived at the school, that bravery disappeared. There were 200 youngsters ready to participate; some were university students, others had jobs, some were older, others very young. The younger ones, like me, had to answer questions. The older ones had to write an essay. Some also had good connections, something I didn't have. I was just a poor boy from the countryside, so I figured I wouldn't stand a chance.

"Just in case, I stayed to wait for the results. That took another three days. Six people were chosen, and I was on the list! I was delighted. They gave us a permission slip for our parents to sign. They had to give their consent. After all, we weren't about to embark on a small mission; we were about to give our lives to the Panchen Lama. We would do as he told us and go where he sent us. Of course it was impossible for me to travel for days to get my parents to fill in the form, so I signed it myself.

"Then something terrible happened. The next day we were to meet the Panchen Lama, but when I arrived, my name had been taken from the list. I still don't know what happened. Maybe somebody had used his connections to replace my name with his own. I wanted to see the Panchen Lama and tell him about this injustice, but I couldn't get close to him. I was standing there, crying, because I was so furious, but they wouldn't let me in. I decided then and there that I would be a member of the mission, no matter what.

"I went home and asked my parents for money. I told them that I had to go to Tibet. I knew that the others would go to school in Shigatse, so I went with my uncle to the city and tried to fly to Lhasa from there. But that turned out to be complicated. At that time, you needed five different documents to be able to buy a plane ticket. I only had my identity card. So I took the bus to Ganzi. There I had some friends, and they gave me some more money, food and clothes, because I had practically nothing. From Ganzi I took a truck. We went with about ten people, peasants from the area. At night we slept by the side of the road. It was very cold.

"After nine days, I made it to Lhasa. For Tibetans this is a big, holy city. I didn't know anybody there. I only knew that one of my former classmates had gone to the university of Lhasa, but I had no address. I was lucky. That night they were showing a movie on the university campus. It was filled with students. When I walked through the entrance, I almost bumped into my friend. He could hardly believe his eyes. I was incredibly filthy; my clothes were full of dust and insects. We first watched the movie and then he gave me shelter. I don't know what would have happened to me if I hadn't found him.

"My friend also knew that the living Buddha from our district was now staying with the chosen students. That gave me hope, because he should know that I had passed the exam. I found a car to take me to Shigatse. There, I saw how happy the others were. They had everything they needed and they were full of confidence about their bright futures. The teachers there were impressed with my perseverance. They had trouble believing that I had come so far, all on my own. But they didn't have my exam paper any more, it had disappeared and the Panchen Lama had strict rules. So they made me retake the exam. I couldn't sleep that night. I was afraid because my Tibetan wasn't so good. When I was young, there were no Tibetan schools. And what would I do if I were refused again? The day of the exam I was sitting by myself in this small room and trembling like a leaf.

"But I got through the tests and was admitted. In 1987, I enrolled to study architecture in Tianjin. Very few people wanted to do this, I don't know why. But I still wasn't good in Tibetan and architecture seemed like a useful subject. We left with a group of 25 students. In Beijing the Panchen Lama received us. "This is your chance, take it," he told us. He had called the authorities in Tianjin, and we received a grand reception, with music and journalists who put our picture in the papers. I studied architectural management. Each student had a specific teacher who took care of us.

"But we only studied for five months until the Panchen Lama called us back to Beijing. We were to start working in his corporation, Gangjian, he said. We set up the headquarters in a building behind the train station. In the beginning I lived in the Panchen Lama's house and I knew his whole family. The Panchen Lama was a man who expected much and it was tiring to work for him. I was in charge of finances and had to bring a report to him every week. We always had to be available. When he called, we went.

"He was very strict and could get really angry at us. When we still lived in Shigatse, he came one day to lecture us. We had had a fight with some people in Shigatse about movie tickets. To punish us, he made us stand in a line for one day and one night. I was often cuffed, because I like to laugh. I also laugh when I'm nervous. So the Panchen Lama was mad at us, and I giggled. He pulled me by the ear, and I still chuckled. That day I was wearing a big pair of yellow pants and in the bright light they looked white. "What kind of foreign clothes are you wearing?" the Panchen Lama roared. "Take that off." So I had to take off my pants while everyone was watching.

"During the time that I worked for Gangjian, I traveled everywhere with him. I was the youngest and people often thought I was a living Buddha. They couldn't imagine that such a young guy could work for such an important leader. During the Panchen Lama's last trip we stayed in Shigatse for 20 days. Some people think that the Panchen Lama knew he was going to die. A few days before he died he gave a picture of himself to the lamas in the monastery as a remembrance.

"That night I had another dream. Many people came to give shawls to the Panchen Lama. This time I had no idea what that meant. At five o'clock in the morning someone woke me up. They told us that the Panchen Lama was ill. A medical team from Beijing was flown in. We were not allowed to see him. They told us that he had heart problems and couldn't talk. So we all waited outside. Around noon the doctors came out. We thought that the Panchen Lama was cured and we were relieved. One of the doctors saw our happy faces and stopped. "The Panchen Lama has passed away," he told us.

"The news made me dizzy and we all burst into tears. When my parents passed on I wasn't as sad as when the Panchen Lama died. The whole night we stayed with his wife to console her. She wanted to throw herself on the body, but we restrained her. She became angry and said, "Now you don't listen to me any more?" Over the following days I became very depressed. I couldn't sleep, nor eat. When I saw those poor people outside the monastery I thought, "Who will take care of them now that there is no Panchen Lama?"

"Completely bereaved, we went back to Beijing, but we were also determined to continue the work of our leader. That is why I am still here. The Development Fund set up 130 projects. I regularly travel to Tibet and try to find funds to help the poor. Many foreign NGOs are interested. There is the Trace Foundation that helps, and I went on a mission with Doctors Without Borders. During one of the snow disasters, I took three doctors to the nomads. The snow reached up to our knees. Afterwards we went back to Xining and collected money and goods. I went back and forth this way five times. The authorities gave us trucks to use, because the nomads lived over seven hundred kilometers away. It was right next to my village, but I didn't even have time to see my family. In that same year I did see how the children in my area didn't go to school. They went with their parents to work. So we got money from the authorities and built a school.

"So that's my life now. Every time there is something new to do. Sometimes it's a flood; other times there is too much snow. I now understand what the Panchen Lama meant when he said, "If we want to develop Tibet, we will have to find very motivated people and we will have to work very hard"."

9.

Monasteries as political battlefields

One letter kept in file attracted much attention. It read: 'Rab Ge: A Buddhist ceremony will be held here. We need meat, hearts and blood from all kinds of animals, four human heads, intestines, pure blood, turbid blood, earth from ruins, the menstrual blood of a widow, the blood of a leper, water from beneath the surface of the earth, earth raised in a whirlwind, brambles growing towards the north, excrement of both dog and man and the boots of a butcher. All these should be sent to Tsechykhang on the 27th. Tsechykhang, the 19th.'

(Chinatibetnews.com, March 21, 2008)

Your travelers have spoken of being beset by hordes of fanatical monks. You may be assured that if ever they were in danger it had nothing to do with religious fanaticism, which does not exist in our country. We are not fanatics, neither our lamas nor our laymen. Buddhism is not hostile to other religions. Such an attitude is alien to both our religion and to the Tibetan character.

(*We Tibetans*, Rinchen Lhamo, 1926)

Buddhism is tolerated in Tibet, and with the more liberal party policy, the Tibetans manage to worship once more. Some of the monasteries have opened up, monks walk around in their robes and paint the golden Buddha statues, and the pilgrims slide along the ground. But it will never be the way it was.

In the old Tibet, being a monk meant having access to the most prestigious jobs in the country, and the Jokhang temple was the holiest place on earth. Every family tried to send at least one child to a lamasery. If your child turned out to be the reincarnation of an important lama, your family was sure to get high status within society. The monastery was also the only place where your child could be educated. Young monks learned how to read and write, practice traditional medicine and Buddhist theory. Since a lot of studying had to be done, the children went as early as possible.

Buddhism actually comes from the Northeast of India and began in the fifth century BC. A prince, Siddhartha, founded it. His parents had told him that he could do whatever he wanted as long as he didn't become a priest. Or course everyone just expected him to inherit his father's throne. All was well, until Siddhartha one day discovered that the people outside the palace were suffering. He decided to leave his riches behind and find a way to end misery. He went into the woods and learned from the spiritual men there, but their beliefs didn't satisfy him and after years of seeking, he sat down under a tree and started to think about his own spirit. That way, he found enlightenment. In his new state, he saw that the causes of suffering were to be found in the way humans think and constantly want things. Siddhartha became the first Buddha.

Buddhism soon turned out to be a religion that easily mixed with others. In Tibet, for instance, people believed in spirits and gods who lived in sacred places. The people worshiped dead kings and performed exorcisms. All of these aspects are still found in Tibetan Buddhism today.

An important part of the belief of Buddhism is the concept of reincarnation. According to its followers, life is a cycle of rebirths. There are six different levels in which you can be born and you try to avoid coming back on one of the lower levels, like an insect, for instance. On the other hand, each soul is likely to go through all stages. To get on with this life cycle, you need to collect as much good karma as you can. You can do this by performing good deeds during your life, or to live as a monk or hermit, devoting yourself to meditation and religious study. The bad things you do will affect your next life. Once you reach enlightenment, you can become a Buddha and you won't need to be reborn again. Living Buddhas are those who have decided to come back to earth anyway so they can help others on their paths. The Dalai Lama and the Panchen Lama are the highest living Buddhas. The first is considered to be the Buddha of Compassion and the latter the Buddha of Wisdom.

Seeking the reincarnation of an important lama or Buddha is a difficult process. Sometimes the dying lama leaves a sign: for instance, he'll look north on his deathbed to the place where he's planning to be reborn. The Dalai Lama has already made it clear that he will be reborn abroad, as long as there is a task for him there. Then there is the oracle, a monk who gets taken over by a spirit who helps out. While in trance, the spirit will predict the future or give advice. When the oracle points to a place, a special delegation goes in that direction and looks for a child of the right age. This child then is expected to recognize people or objects from his former life. This process can take a long time; after the demise of the Panchen Lama, the search party looked for five years. If the monks are satisfied with the candidate, the child will be taken back to the monastery.

The Dalai Lama writes in his autobiography about the death and subsequent meeting with the reincarnation of his senior tutor, Ling Rinpoche. "He entered a coma from which he never emerged and died on 25 December 1983. But his body did not begin to decay until 13 days after he was pronounced dead, despite the hot climate. It was as if he still inhabited his body, even though clinically it was without life. ... Ling Rinpoche's reincarnation has since been found, and he is presently a very bright and naughty boy of three. His discovery was one of those where the child clearly recognizes a member of the search party. Despite his being only 18 months old, he actually called the person by name and went forward to him, smiling. Subsequently he correctly identified several others of his predecessor's acquaintances. ... When I received the boy at my residence and he was brought to the door, he acted just like his predecessor had done. It was plain that he remembered his way around."

In the new Tibet, however, there is no more deep religious study, and the process of finding reincarnations has become a political game. The Chinese authorities give heaps of money to rebuild the monasteries; after all, they attract tourists. The Chinese media love to report on the restorations that take place. China completely restored the Potala, the palace of the Dalai Lama, and the Ganden monastery, the biggest in Tibet, got a new golden roof with 23 kilos of gold. But money always comes with oppression, because the authorities also feel that religion is something dangerous that needs tight control.

Because of the work of the Dalai Lama in India, the monasteries have become political battlefields. Monks live under strict restrictions. The authorities decide how many monks can join a monastery and each candidate has to go through a bureaucratic process – not that the Tibetans always listen. In the provinces, where security is not as tight, extra members and children – who are forbidden to become monks until they turn 18 – manage to get in anyway. As soon as a monastery or a Buddhist teacher becomes too powerful, the authorities start a campaign. Anyone who doesn't have the right papers gets thrown out and the official monks are put through another round of political indoctrination.

Redi, head of the Tibetan People's Congress, is in favor of these campaigns. "Last year, we gave patriotic education to 30,000 lamas in 900 temples. We did this in order to guarantee the freedom of religion. During the Cultural Revolution, this policy was not well implemented, but, as you know, we now have religious freedom again. Nonetheless, the situation keeps getting out of hand. This is because of the infiltration of the Dalai Lama, so some re-education is necessary. In every country, people need to love their state, and monks and nuns are also people."

Redi thinks that the campaigns are very successful. "With these lessons, the lamas get better insight into the laws. The system's management has improved too. Before, there was chaos. The big monasteries didn't even know how many monks they had. Only a few lamas had any idea what their income and expenses were. Now there is a standardized accounting system and the monks can become members of the Democratic Committee, which takes care of the daily management of the institution. During the campaigns we have found criminals and we expelled them from the temples. I don't understand why Westerners are so interested in these campaigns. They accuse us of curtailing freedom of religion. But I would like to know: which country lets people commit crimes in the name of religion? Why are the Americans allowed to ban sects and the Japanese can put a sect leader on trial, but the Chinese can't?"

The monks are obviously less enthusiastic about the Democratic Committee and the campaigns. The same monastery that got the golden roof was closed for several months after the monks protested against the rules of the Democratic Committee; the leaders wanted to get rid of the ancient paintings of the Dalai Lama. Eyewitnesses told the Western media that they had seen two army trucks carrying wounded monks pass by on their way to the hospital. According to an eyewitness, armed soldiers came with a list of 92 names, all monks who had to be expelled from the monastery. The lamas, for their part, are the most daring when it comes to speaking up or organizing demonstrations. Because it's impossible to reform them, jailed monks and nuns get the harshest treatment.

The authorities also like to control the reincarnations of high lamas. After all, having a three-year-old religious leader grow up under Chinese influence is a great opportunity to keep the Tibetan people in line. These boys serve as propaganda material. One of the favorites of the media used to be the young Lama of the White Sect of Lamaism. When the boy was 12, the authorities gave the living Buddha a brand new Toyota 4500 as a present to celebrate the 30th anniversary of the Tibetan Autonomous Region. "We are sure that the present will inspire the young Buddha to more prayers," a magazine in Beijing reported. It was serious. The magazine went on to proudly state that the young lama was the first Tibetan ever to get a car from the Chinese government. A few years before that, the living Buddha stood next to Chinese president Jiang Zemin and watched the celebrations for Chinese National Day. The president told the boy to study hard, stay healthy, and be religious and patriotic towards China. According to the Chinese media, the boy had answered by proclaiming, "Long live the People's Republic of China!"

However, when the Chinese government decided to take over the search for the new Panchen Lama, even Tibetans in China thought they went too far. After the search party had looked for boys for over five years, it presented four candidates. The head of the group then sent two messages: one to the authorities in Beijing and one secretly to the Dalai Lama. The Communist Party, which had promised to respect the choice of the Tibetans, didn't have time to look into the matter – the message arrived during the session of the People's Congress, the biggest political showcase of the year. The Dalai Lama did take the matter into immediate consideration and approved the name of the boy that the committee in Tibet had chosen.

The Chinese were furious. They declared that, because of historical reasons, they were the ones that had the right to approve the reincarnation. The head of the search committee was jailed for "leaking state secrets" and the boy chosen by the Dalai Lama disappeared. The reincarnation, named Gedhun Choekyi Nyima, and his parents were soon added to Amnesty International's list of missing people. Whenever Western diplomats ask about the Gedhun, the authorities refuse to show him, and declare that the boy is safe. They have to protect him, they say, so he won't be "kidnapped by separatists." They also try to convince the world that the Gedhun is not the right candidate. "To choose this boy would be an insult to the Buddha," Xinhua stated. According to the Chinese press, the boy had once drowned a dog and his parents had lied about his date of birth. But finding another candidate proved to be an almost impossible task. First the Chinese officials called all the high lamas to Beijing. In a heavily guarded military hotel they were told to make their choice, but the lamas immediately started to sabotage the process: they declared that they had to go back to Tibet to carry out some rituals before they could decide on a reincarnation. They said that they felt there was no religious leader available who could take this decision. They were told to hurry. Eventually a very sad picture was published on the front page of the *China Daily*. Chinese party leaders are all sitting rather uncomfortably in the front row. Behind them stand a row of lamas, none of them smiling. One of the monks later managed to talk to the foreign press. "We didn't have a choice," he said. "We were forced to do this, but I suppose it's better to have two Panchen Lamas than none at all." After all, it wouldn't be the first time that there were rival reincarnations in Tibet.

In the end the lamas held a lottery among the three remaining candidates, a ceremony which took place in the Panchen's monastery. A student told me how the authorities gathered some Tibetans, told them to wear their best clothes and cheer for the new Panchen Lama, all for the benefit of another historical picture to be published all over China. The Chinese choice was then taken to Beijing, where he carried out his first rites in the Xihuang temple, accompanied by the last Panchen Lama's mother. There he stays, safely under the protection of the Chinese. An official portrait was made of him to hang in the temples of Tibet. According to the media, the young man now spends his days reading Buddhist texts, but he also likes to play on his computer.

In Tibet I didn't hear any monks complain about their situation; they wouldn't dare. But they do speak up about their second concern, the loss of their religious knowledge. The most important religious leaders are now all in India and daily life in the monastery, as the next monk describes it, leaves little time for studies.

But Buddhism in Tibet has known worse times. According to Buddhists, the religion went through a much more difficult period at the beginning of the last century. But throughout history, the religion has always adapted itself to new circumstances. The fact that there are still boys like Pemba, who at the age of 16 ran away to India just to study Buddhism, should be an encouragement to the leaders.

In other Asian countries it's hard to find this kind of dedication. The Taiwanese Buddhist Society asked for help from the Dalai Lama when they saw their public slipping away. He visited the island at the same time the Buddhist leaders were exhibiting a tooth that is supposed to have belonged to the first Buddha. The Taiwanese leaders were trying to get Westernized Chinese back onto the religious path. This is difficult. Everywhere in Asia, young people prefer Hollywood movies to Buddhist rituals. Only in Tibet is there no such trend. The more the Chinese forbid it, the more the people turn to the temples. Buddhism has become the number one path of resistance. After all, nothing is as convincing as a religious martyr.

NEMA TSERING, MONK IN THE JOKHANG TEMPLE

Nema Tsering presents a yellow name card on which the name of his institute – the Jokhang temple – is written in golden letters. Nema works at the tourist reception, a small room above the entrance to Tibet's most famous temple. Together with three other young colleagues he sells tickets to visitors. While he talks and laughs, snow starts falling outside. The monk serves us cups of hot water so we can all keep warm. It's all really cozy until a heavy-breathing Chinese guide comes stomping up the stairs. She's clearly another victim of altitude sickness, a fact which seems to irritate her immensely. The guide wants to use old entry tickets. Nema smiles and nods, then refuses politely.

"I always wanted to join the monastery, because I wanted to study culture. I loved our traditions and of course I was raised to be a Buddhist. Most culture in Tibet has a religious background and so the best teachers are in the monasteries. When I was 17 years old, I ran away from home. It was the summer holiday and I told my parents that I was going to Lhasa to visit family, but in fact I was planning to become a monk.

"I had heard that here there was a chance for me to get in. This was because the Panchen Lama, our religious leader, visited the Jokhang and saw that there were not enough monks to do the work. He asked the leaders in Beijing for permission to add 16 more places. I had a teacher who introduced me, and that's how I got a spot. We first had to pass an exam and the authorities in the city had to approve my nomination. After that there was a period of two years while I wasn't yet allowed to live in the monastery, but the authorities inspected my behavior. In the beginning we had to clean the square in front of the temple – that was our task. At that time there was no tar, so every morning we raked the sand. Later on we were allowed to live in the temple.

"My parents were very happy when they heard that I had become a monk. In the old Tibet you could do this when you were very young. The people used to think 'the younger the better', because then you would have more time to study. But nowadays we have to go to school first. Then, when you're 18, you can choose for yourself what you want to do.

"We are 120 monks here; some don't have a permit to stay in Lhasa even if they have been here for ten years already. It's difficult if you don't have a license. For instance, you have to pay for the doctor and you can't buy subsidized food. I do have permission and this is why the state pays me a salary of 160 yuan a month. That's not a lot because a good pair of shoes costs 200 yuan, but we don't need much. We cook ourselves a little *tsampa* and drink yak butter tea, and that's enough. A monk doesn't need to be rich, but it's also not good to be too poor. Some people think that being a Buddhist means that you're not allowed to possess anything and that you spend your time meditating in an icy cold cave. But our religious doctrine doesn't state that at all. Those people who want to live soberly do this because they want to.

"The monks who don't have permission to live here get a salary from the monastery, paid out of the ticket money. The monastery earns about 20,000 yuan a year for selling these tickets; that's just enough to keep up the buildings around here. We ask for financial help whenever we need to restore the statues, so for those projects we get money from the state.

"Life in the monastery is different from what I expected. I don't get much time to study, we are too busy managing the temple. Not that I'm complaining, I'm already happy that I have a place. In winter, from November through March, many Tibetans come on pilgrimages. In those months it's too cold for the farmers to work on the land, so they have time to come here. We have to receive them and accept their donations, and they have a lot of questions we have to answer. In summer, from April to October, when other monks have time to study, we are busy with the tourists. Tourists are less work than the pilgrims, because most of them bring their own guides. But we do have to be here at the office. So throughout the whole year we only have a few hours a day to learn our Buddhist texts.

"Political studies? Yes, sure, we have those all the time. First we did a course on socialism. Last year, we spent four months on lessons of patriotism. Every afternoon we read four books: the law, the history of Tibet, and ways to counter separatism. After that we had an exam. We all passed, because those who didn't score high enough had to do the course all over again until their marks had improved. We also watched the news every night. That's very interesting, because there we can see how complicated the world is and what problems there are.

"Traditionally we believe that the Dalai Lama represents the sun and the Panchen Lama the moon. I always knew that the Dalai Lama lived in India, but that didn't seem strange to me at all. We always thought of India as Tibet's big brother. Whenever we saw foreigners we always thought that they were Indians. Nowadays we know better. We finished all our lessons. The demonstrations in 1987? I don't remember. It was in all the newspapers. Why don't you read those if you want to know what happened?

"We have a shortage of Buddhist teachers. During the Cultural Revolution no new ones were educated, so we only have two left. One is on a pilgrimage, so right now we are depending on our 84-year-old master. Sometimes he still reads to us until ten o'clock at night, even though his eyes are bothering him and he is not healthy any more. We feel really sorry for him, but he knows that if he dies there will be no one to replace him.

"Yes, we believe in reincarnation. I personally never saw any proof but there are many stories. When I was small my mother used to tell me that in her village a girl had died before she had a chance to finish reading one of her books. The grieving mother always kept the book. After ten years another child came by and she asked if she could have her old book back, because she hadn't had a chance to finish it. She knew exactly on which page she had stopped reading in her last life.

"There are many stories that prove our beliefs, but here in the monastery, there is no mystery. We don't know how to go back to our former lives, for instance. Those are very special skills. You have to reach a very advanced stage in your meditation. I don't think there are any teachers left in Tibet who know how to do these things.

"Our religion is also becoming more corrupted. There is nobody to control anything, so anyone can pretend to be a religious leader. Here in Lhasa there are people who put on monks' robes and start to ask for money on the street for their supposed monastery. During the pilgrimages we have to guard the statues. Sometimes, if you don't pay attention, relics get stolen. A golden crown, for example, or a religious ornament. In the old days that would have been impossible, people wouldn't have done this. Nowadays they care too much about money. Money has become a goal in life, as opposed to a means. But at the same time those people feel empty. There are more and more mentally disturbed people in Lhasa. People don't have inner peace any more. In Tibet we say if you sow beans you will harvest beans.

"Some Westerners want to come and study here. We tell them that Tibet is a good place to meditate, because there are many sacred spots, but if they want to learn anything they are in the wrong place. I have heard that in other countries there are very good schools for Buddhism. A few years ago there was still a living Buddha here who would give a lecture about Buddhism twice a year, but he has died too.

"Generally speaking, you have to spend your whole life, or at least until you are 60 years old, studying and meditating before you can reach a higher spiritual level. We call this tandrik. But I don't think I will reach it in my time. Maybe I'll do better during my next life."

PEMBA, THE RUNAWAY MONK

From his bench in the Reception Center, we take Pemba to the restaurant in my hotel. There, he refuses to eat or drink anything. In the end we serve him tea, which he slurps up only after much insisting from our side. Then, in a high child's voice, he bursts out, "There is no freedom in the monasteries. We can't even hang a picture of His Holiness. They came to check on us all the time." The host of the restaurant, a robust Tibetan woman in her thirties, joins us to listen to the story, but Pemba looks at her, shocked, and stops talking. The woman fondly squeezes his shoulder and disappears back into the kitchen.

"I joined the monastery when I was 11 years old. It went like this: when I was small, I had an infection on my navel. A visiting lama from one of the other villages saw me and told my parents, 'This is a special child. You have to keep him clean and take care that he becomes a monk.' Since I was a small child I had this feeling that I wanted to serve society and the world. There was no problem for me to live in the monastery, because my brother was also a monk. There were seven children in our family and two of us joined. The Chinese don't want you to become a monk until you're 18. They always told us that religion is not good for children and not good for society. They said I was much too young, but they didn't throw me out either. That has changed now. These last few years they have started to check the ages of the monks much more closely.

"For my admission, there was a welcoming ceremony. My parents gave tea and food to all the monks. The two highest lamas ran the monastery, we didn't have a Democratic Committee. There were no cadres in our monastery either. But the lamas did need permission from the local authorities for whatever they wanted to do. Sometimes they would come and check if we had Dalai Lama posters. These inspectors were always the same people, two Chinese and a Tibetan. They would come a few times a month, when you didn't expect them, and search all our rooms for forbidden documents. They never found any. Not that we didn't have anything forbidden, but we could always see the inspectors coming from far away and would have time enough to hide all the pictures of His Holiness before they made it to the front gate. When they were gone we would put everything back.

"Before I became a monk I had never been to school. There was a small school a few hours away from my village, but you had to pay tuition and my parents didn't have money. My father taught me to read and write a little. He had been a monk himself, but the Chinese had expelled him and forced him to become a normal civilian. My parents told me how the Chinese revolutionaries had destroyed my monastery, but they never said why this had happened. They also said that His Holiness was in India, and as a small boy I always wanted to know why our leader wasn't with us. Then they would answer, 'Because the Chinese forced him to leave.' But I knew nothing about politics; they never talked about independence or ideas like that.

"In the beginning I loved the life in the monastery. Every day there were religious studies. My brother also taught me, and we studied the whole day. But trouble started when the authorities started a patriotic campaign. A group of Chinese and Tibetans came to live with us for two months. Every day we had to study their documents which criticized His Holiness. The Chinese said that if we didn't accept these lessons we would be punished. At the end there was an oral exam and finally we had to sign a document against His Holiness. That went too far, I refused to do that. His Holiness is the most important man in the lives of the Tibetans; how could we let him down? My friends all signed but I didn't. I said, 'Do what you want, throw me in jail, but I do not agree with this document.' The Chinese have always looked down on us and I thought that if I signed, it would show that they were right and that we were really weak.

"My friends and my brother all did sign their names. My brother really had no choice; he was one of the leaders of the monastery. I understood that. If we all refused, everybody would be thrown out and the monastery would have been empty. That would have made me sad. Of course the Chinese could throw everybody out; they don't care. As far as they're concerned, anyone who wants to go can leave immediately. I had to put my thumbprint under a document that stated that I would leave the monastery. I had to give back my monk's robes and was not allowed to organize any religious activities.

"And so I went back home. It was Tibetan New Year and I had already decided that I had better run away to India. My parents agreed. 'At least you will be able to study there,' they said. I left for Lhasa and once there I bought permission to travel to the border. I told the authorities in Lhasa that I had family in Nepal whom I wanted to visit. This was in fact true, I even had pictures of the family. In Lhasa they didn't know that I had been expelled from the monastery; if they had known, they would never have let me go.

"It was not difficult to catch the bus to the Nepalese border. There, I paid a merchant to take me to the other side. He gave me Nepalese clothes and put me on a bus inbetween Nepalese children. He charged 1,000 yuan to smuggle me over. In Nepal I went to the Refugee Reception Center. I was very lonely there, I didn't talk much with the others. There were many people, from all districts, and I didn't understand their dialects. But I didn't get homesick, because I was determined to study Buddhism, so being far away from home didn't make me unhappy.

"After two weeks I came to Dharamsala. I'm so happy to be here. It's like a dream, all these pictures of His Holiness everywhere. At the Reception Center they told me that it would not be a problem to get a place in one of the Tibetan monasteries.

"I will stay here until Tibet is independent or until His Holiness goes back. I'm sure that His Holiness will soon return to an independent Tibet. What? Autonomy? The Dalai Lama doesn't ask for independence? No, I didn't know that. Can I go now?"

10.

SPIRITS IN THE MOUNTAINS

Some of your writers have it that we are a people sunk in superstition. We are not so. I cannot see that we are more superstitious than you are. In some ways we are less so. We believe in our religion. That is not superstition. You believe in yours. But many of you seem to believe in strange things which are outside your religion. I have heard about your spiritualistic seances, and I have seen books with photographs supposed to be of the spirits of the dead. ... We do not seek contact with spirits, as you do in your spiritualistic seances. We believe that nothing but harm can come from contact with them. We do not believe, for instance, that the spirit of a departed friend or relative can be of assistance to the living. ... Contact with the dead, however, does occur occasionally. Sometimes the dead try to draw the living after them. This is where some great affection existed, the dead desiring their loved ones to join them. Sometimes it happens when not affection but hatred is there, the dead having suffered some great injustice.

It is not only the living people to which the thoughts of the dead are apt to turn, but also to material objects they were especially attached to in life; and so it is that no Tibetan will knowingly use things that were of special moment to someone who has died.

In all these cases where contact with the dead has occurred, the lamas are called in. They hold the appropriate service and the spirit of the dead departs, leaving the living in peace. Discarnate spirits are also said to disport themselves in wood and glade and ravine. They dance as we do, round-dances. And here and there you may see, in some secluded place, the circle their feet have trodden in the grass. If a human being comes upon them they disappear. But not always. ...

Apart from the spirits of the dead, there are other spirits which can trouble mankind. There is, for instance, Terang-gungchi. No one has seen any more of this spirit than his footsteps in the snow. It is the footprint of a human child two or three years old. And he has only one foot. He delights in confusing people's affairs. It is he who leads people to foolish actions.

(*We Tibetans,* Rinchen Lhamo, 1926)

The Tibetans have a colorful culture that is based on their religion and beliefs. Maintaining the mysteries of their country is for many as important as the preservation of the Buddhist religion itself. In Tibet, you find stories about spirits and demons at every level of society. According to the people, the mountaintops are inhabited by all kinds of phantoms and monsters like the Yeti, the abominable snowman. Refugees like to think that spirits protect them during their long marches through the snow, and an important part of Tibetan traditional medicine is based on liberating people from evil supernatural beings. Funerals are spiritual gatherings where the dead are cut up into pieces and put on mountaintops so that buzzards take the deceased to heaven.

Mysteries are not only for the common or uneducated. The Dalai Lama also believes in them. He states in his autobiography that he doesn't possess any supernatural abilities, but that is mostly because he never had time to develop any. After more than 50 years of traveling around the world, the highest lama has become a modern politician, but he also consults the state oracle before he decides on any major issue.

The members of the government in Dharamsala, contemporary people who were raised outside Tibet and spend most of their time practicing democracy, also believe in the 'Dharma protector', as they call the oracle. The *kuten*, or the bodily base of the Nechung – the god that protects the government – automatically becomes a vice-minister.

In his autobiography, the Dalai Lama explains. "For hundreds of years now, it has been traditional for the Dalai Lama, and the Government, to consult Nechung during the New Year festivals. In addition, he might well be called upon at other times if either have specific queries. I myself have dealings with him several times a year. This may sound far-fetched to 20th-century Western readers. Even some Tibetans, mostly those who consider themselves 'progressive', have misgivings about my continued use of this ancient method of intelligence-gathering. But I do so for the simple reason that as I look back over the many occasions when I have asked questions of the oracle, on each one of them time has proven that his answer was correct. This is not to say that I rely solely on the oracle's advice. I do not. I seek his opinion in the same way as I seek the opinion of my Cabinet and just as I seek the opinion of my own conscience. I consider the gods to be my 'upper house'. The Kashag constitutes my lower house. Like any other leader, I consult both before making a decision on affairs of state. And sometimes, in addition to Nechung's counsel, I also take into consideration certain prophecies."

The spirits appear in every aspect of Tibetan culture. Tibetan traditional dancing is often carried out to chase away evil demons. Tibet's most famous dance is called Cham. It's a ritual carried out by monks and nuns and is about the oppression of wicked ghosts. The dancers wear colorful masks and dance to heavy music of drums and long horns. The major character is the unmasked lama of the Black Hat sect. The monks, who play protective deities, surround him. The other focal point of the dance is the lingam, a human form that has evil spirits in it. Anthropologists have given all kinds of interpretations to the performance. Some say that the lama represents the monk who killed Lang Dharma, an anti-Buddhist king, and that the ritual shows the spreading of Buddhism in Tibet. Others see Cham as a metaphor for the slow process of controlling one's ego, the final goal of Buddhism.

Then there is the songwriting. Tibetans always sing, whether knotting carpets or working on the land. Some years ago some nuns were harshly punished because they wouldn't stop singing about Tibet's independence, even after they had been put in jail. There used to be minstrels who would travel around entertaining the people. The songs are often ironic and political, while others have clear religious themes. There is one song, for instance, that describes an aristocratic woman who exposes herself to burning incense, hoping that will make her give birth to the next Dalai Lama.

The miracles of Tibet also attract scientists. In his autobiography the Dalai Lama describes experiments carried out by American doctors. These traveled to India to examine meditating monks. The monks were skilled in a certain kind of yoga. They were said to be able to turn off their usual senses, like smell and sight, and reach a broader level of consciousness which is comparable to the final stage of life right before dying. The doctors discovered that as soon as the monks entered their trance, their body temperature increased by ten degrees. This way they were able to stay in the snow the whole night without freezing. The bodies of the monks were so hot that they could be covered with wet sheets and their bodies would dry them within a quarter of an hour.

The Tibetans in Dharamsala work hard to keep all aspects of their culture alive. Statue making, carpet knotting, teaching of meditation; Tibetan culture blooms in the Indian mountains. The exiles wear traditional clothes and set up workshops where newly arrived refugees learn arts and crafts. The inhabitants of McLeod believe in their mysteries, but they also have an earthly reason to hold onto their culture; it's what keeps them together.

The preservation of the Tibetan culture is, after all, also a political issue. The Tibetans think that as soon as Tibet becomes independent, they can go back and teach the old traditions to the people who stayed behind and lost their culture. Even if there are no more revolutionaries to smash the monasteries, the culture in Tibet has been destroyed in a more subtle way, they say. Due to the influx of Chinese immigrants and the biased educational system, the Tibetans are becoming more and more Chinese.

It's true that culture in Tibet itself is a sorry affair. Even though cultural events are not forbidden, they don't thrive either. Instead you find people who with great difficulty try to save what they can. In Beijing I met a former doctor of the Panchen Lama. He told me how it was impossible for him to treat patients the traditional way during the Cultural Revolution. Mao Zedong promoted the traditional Chinese medicine, but branded the Tibetan knowledge as superstition. When the Panchen Lama became old and ill, he wanted to see a Tibetan doctor, but by that time it was difficult to find one. The young doctors didn't know anything about their own natural remedies, as a whole generation had not been taught this knowledge. So the Tibetans made all the old doctors pass an exam, and the best one was taken to Beijing to take care of the lama.

The doctor told me that since the Panchen Lama passed away, he had been taking care of the monks in the Buddhist Study Center in Beijing. He traveled to Inner Mongolia, where people also believe in his cures. The old physician dreamed of starting up a hospital in his place of birth, Qinghai, and teaching young doctors the old cures. But there was no money and the government didn't subsidize those kinds of projects, he said. The only Chinese who were interested in his Tibetan herbs were some businessmen who wanted to sell the strange-looking herbal balls as a wonder cure in an amusement park. In Dharamsala, on the other hand, there is a new hospital paid for by the community. Students major in traditional medicine and are then put to work. They talk about their jobs with enthusiasm. Not only sick Tibetans but also Indians and Westerners seek treatment.

The central government in Beijing only shows interest in Tibetan culture when it serves as propaganda. Having Tibetan dancers in colorful costumes perform at state banquets is meant to show what a big happy family the Han Chinese and the minorities are. After the Hollywood movies about Heinrich Harrer and the Dalai Lama came out, a true cultural battle ensued between the two sides. China spent millions filming its own version of Tibetan history in lavish productions. Instead of the hiking Austrian, the main character was a Chinese princess who married a Tibetan king and traveled to his region. Much of the historical claim that China has over Tibet is based on this marriage, never mind that the same king also married a Nepalese and a few Tibetan women.

There is a wide discrepancy between what the Chinese authorities and the Tibetans think is important about their culture. The Chinese tend to look at the outside. They spend millions restoring the Potala Palace and gilding the Buddha statues. The Tibetans, on the other hand, find the religious aspect more important. Without freedom of religion, there is no way for cultural values to be preserved. For the Tibetans, a monastery is not complete without the Dalai Lama's picture. And the renovated Potala is nothing but an empty shell without the Buddha himself. It's nice for the foreigners – I was amazed to see this dark, bare place and imagined the Dalai Lama growing up in these surroundings. But for the Tibetans, the man himself is much more important than the statues. In Dharamsala the Dalai Lama lives in a Western villa and the monks meditate, not in their own monasteries in the sacred mountains, but in low brick houses. There, they are allowed to do as they please, pray as much as they want and hang as many posters of His Holiness as they have space for. As a consequence, if you want so see mystery, you have to travel to the Indian mountains.

THUPTEN NGODUP, THE STATE ORACLE

Karma is sweating and trembling. "This is a very important man. It makes me nervous to translate for him," he admits. Thupten Ngodup, medium for the Nechung state oracle, is ordering some Coca-Cola. Then he joins us in the small square room in the monastery in McLeod. During the day, the state oracle is an affable monk, his skin shiny and healthy. Once in a while – "The last time I was in a trance? That was yesterday. The advisors of His Holiness wanted to know something" – his body is taken over by the spirit of Nechung, the protector of the Tibetans.

The day before I meet him, I watch the Hollywood film version of his predecessor. In the movie *Kundun*, which you can see in McLeod in a small, dark video room where the volume is turned up so high that it becomes impossible to understand, I see a giant man wearing an even bigger headdress. He is lying in a blanket which is carried by monks. The headdress alone weighs 40 kilos and if the oracle wasn't in a trance it could break his neck. He wears a costume that is just as sensational as the headdress, and is made up of different layers of cloth. On his chest hangs a mirror with mystifying signs. Before the ceremony starts, the monks also add a kind of harness with flags on his back. Thus dressed, the medium, or *kuten*, can hardly walk, but once the prayers and chanting start and the deity appears, the oracle moves and dances like a wild man, all the while muttering strange cries.

The Dalai Lama describes him in his autobiography. "The volcanic energy of the deity can barely be contained within the earthly frailty of the *kuten*, who moves and gestures as if his body were made of rubber and driven by a coiled spring of enormous power. There follows an interchange between Nechung and myself, where he makes ritual offerings to me. I then ask any personal questions I have for him. After replying, he returns to his stool and listens to questions put by members of the Government. Before giving answers to these the *kuten* begins to dance again, thrashing his sword above his head. He looks like a magnificent, fierce Tibetan warrior chieftain of old."

After the dance, the Dalai Lama or others continue their questioning. "Flee tonight," he told the religious leader in 1959.

"The fact that I'm an oracle doesn't mean that I have supernatural powers. Except when I'm in a trance; then it's different. In daily life, I'm just an ordinary monk. I'm a medium, no more. We had many oracles in the old Tibet. Sometimes the possession would go from father to son, but this is not the case with the Nechung oracle. Nechung always chooses somebody else. You also don't have to be a monk to be possessed by this deity. In the past it also chose normal people like government officials. However, the last two *kutens* of Nechung were both monks. I think Nechung chooses people who have good karma and who pray a lot. You also need clear veins so that the spirit can enter easily. It's like a light wind. Nechung always goes into a man because he is a male spirit. When there is a female deity, she can only possess a female body.

"When I was a child I always felt very close to the Dharma Protector. I felt that I had a very special relationship with him. After the death of the last medium I dreamt a few times about the trance. It wasn't me who was in a trance; the person looked more like the last *kuten*. Other times it was impossible to recognize him. Once I had a dream of a long stairway full of monkeys. According to our religion this has something to do with Nechung.

"Apart from these signs I had a normal youth. My father was a descendant of the famous Ngagpa family who were specialized in tantra. He was very good at carrying out rituals. He always told me that it was his dream to be blessed by His Holiness and then spend the rest of his life like a hermit. The Chinese oppressed my family, just like they did everybody else. I saw how the Tibetans were punished and my grandfather was put in jail. I remember the day he was released. I was four or five years old and we were starving. It was the beginning of the Cultural Revolution.

"After my grandfather came back, we fled to Bhutan, and from there we traveled to India. Here I couldn't go to school immediately. The Children's Village was for orphans, not for children who were here with their parents, and my parents didn't want to send me far away. So I helped building roads.

"Here in India I saw the Tibetan monasteries, and it seemed like a good idea to join. As a child I was already interested in religion and I always wanted to be a monk. One of my uncles was also a monk and my father agreed. At that time the buildings were not as nice as they are now. The Gadong was still in the same building as the Drechung Monastery. Later they became two different institutions, just like in Tibet. After I joined, I studied rituals and eventually I became a ritual leader. I was 31 years old when I was discovered; that was in 1987. My predecessor had been dead for three years. On the 31st of March we have a special day for the Nechung oracle, and we kept on celebrating that even when there was no *kuten*. So it was a little sad, people came to the monastery here but there was nothing to see. His Holiness had written a special prayer for the occasion, to make the oracle come back soon.

"The day before the first trance I was feeling really sad. I felt off-balance and in a bad mood. When I heard that visitors were coming over to perform rituals, I became scared and I felt self-conscious. The day before I had a strange kind of headache. That day, His Holiness gave a lecture and I felt a very strong desire to walk to his throne. So I started to wonder if I wasn't becoming a medium. Afterwards I went to pray to the Buddha, saying that if this was true, he could take away the last obstacles. I wanted to serve the Dharma and Tibet as well as I could. To be the medium for the state oracle is not a normal duty, it's a responsibility of national proportions.

"There were lamas and monks who had come from the Drepung Monastery in southern India. They had visited His Holiness and after that they came here to receive Nechung's blessing, as if there were a real *kuten*. During the first part of the ceremony I went to put an incense pot in front of Nechung's throne. All of a sudden I couldn't leave the hall. It was as if a giant power was pinning me down. I could not take a single step. After a long struggle, I managed to leave through a back door and join the rest of the monks. When the lamas went into Nechung's hall and said their prayers, the trance came to me. I don't really remember, but I do know that my heart started beating quickly and my surroundings became blurred. I started to tremble; it was as if I had been electrocuted. I had no more control over my body. The trance is like a dream that you can't remember the next day but you do know that you had it. It's very scary.

"That first time was very short, it only lasted a few minutes. Nevertheless, the high lamas of the monastery reported it to the Department of Culture and Religion. Some government officials came to look at me and do some tests. They could send me into a trance by carrying out some rituals. When they were satisfied they sent me to His Holiness. He asked me all kinds of questions, like what kind of signals I received, and about my dreams. After that he advised me to go into retreat.

"Nowadays, I am consulted a few times a month. There isn't really a set time. His Holiness and the government ask for the oracle whenever they need it. Normal people can also ask questions if they have permission from the bureau. A few times a year I do a public trance. Everybody can come to that. People want to know all kinds of things; which doctor they should go to or who they should choose as a business partner. The best advice that Nechung ever gave is that His Holiness should follow the Middle Road. He also emphasizes that we shouldn't fight among each other, as we need to stay united. It's up to the Tibetans to listen to Nechung or not.

"The Chinese propaganda always tells lies about me. They made a documentary called *The Dalai Lama* in which they used images of me in trance which the BBC had made. They used those images to portray the oracle in 1959, but I wasn't a *kuten* at that time, it was my predecessor. They also say that the oracle sacrifices blood and human skin to the Dalai Lama. None of that is true. The scene in the movie that is supposed to prove this is really blurry. They also show so-called documents that are supposed to be proof of these things, but the Chinese wrote those themselves.

"The Chinese don't believe in Buddhism, they don't know what religion is. So it's normal that they can't understand religious appearances like the oracle. That's why they say that Nechung is just superstition. For us, on the other hand, it's part of life. We don't need scientific proof that Nechung exists, we know he helps us. We have our Buddhist scriptures and structure as our basis. It's what makes us strong."

TSERING THACKCHOE, THE DOCTOR

"Last year I met an Indian woman who had psychological problems. She had spent three months in a mental institution, but that hadn't helped at all. Then someone advised her to see a Tibetan doctor and so she ended up with me. We also have a clinic in Delhi and we treat many Indian patients there."

Tsering speaks loudly and clearly in fluent English. He's got square glasses and pearly white teeth. Tsering lives in a small room in the hospital in McLeod. We try our best to keep some very persistent flies out of our tea. Tsering's enthusiasm is in complete contrast to the sad Tibetan doctor I spoke with in Beijing. The young physician doesn't know all theories by heart, so every now and then he disappears behind a curtain and comes back with another 1000-year-old document. Searching through these, he explains more about Tibet's traditional form of medicine than I ever learned in Tibet or in China.

"The first time I treated this Indian woman, she was very aggressive and she threw objects at me. She came with a Hindu man who tried to restrain her all the time. My first impression was that she had been poisoned, because her eyes turned in a strange way. But when I held her middle finger, I could feel that a spirit possessed her. I beat her and asked questions, but she refused to answer. After I burned some incense, she calmed down. I told her to come back the next night so I could perform a special ritual.

"At first she didn't want to come back, because the spirit in her didn't trust the situation. But the man brought her anyway. Because of my rituals, the spirit was forced to answer my questions. I talked with her in Hindi. She told me that she was the ghost of a woman who had been murdered by her husband, because this man had a girlfriend. She had come back and taken possession of this body so she could kill the husband. I told her to leave the body of this poor, innocent woman. She refused. So I started to beat her with a hot hammer. After that I gave the woman some traditional medicine. Now the ghost is gone. I recently met the patient, and she is very happy now.

"During our study, we learn to recognize different spirits. For people with mental problems, there are all kinds of cures, medicines and rituals. Not every person with a mental problem is possessed by a spirit; sometimes a person is just traumatized. Like the young Tibetan men who have been in prison, for instance. For them you don't need to do rituals, you just give them advice. I tell them, 'You are here now, and His Holiness shall bless you. You have done a lot for your country so don't worry, Tibet will become independent.' Those kinds of traumas are easy to cure. Tibetans are very religious and that helps.

"I grew up close to Mount Everest; my family still lives there. I started to go to school when I was seven years old. In my spare time, I would take care of the animals. In a faraway village like ours there was no electricity. The Chinese would come by once in a while to show us movies about war. We didn't understand these; we could just make out that the Chinese soldiers always won. Some Tibetan youngsters in the village believed these stories. It was like a fashion in our village to wear pins with Mao Zedong's portrait and to sing Chinese songs. At school we studied Mao's writing, and that was very interesting. It was about how you should take care of yourself and how you should treat others. Everybody had flags and posters of Mao at home, so it was normal that the young people learned from this. Our parents didn't know anything about politics, so we never knew anything about Mao's bad side and the destruction during the Cultural Revolution. The Chinese also gave us all kinds of things. Farmers, who had to pay taxes to landowners before, now got a plot of land and could keep everything they harvested. Those kinds of people are not very educated, so it's easy to convince them.

"I heard from the nomads that you could go to India and study for free and that the schools here had much better facilities. Our school in Tibet was also free, but we learned little. I had an aunt who lived in Nepal and who used to tell us about children getting a blessing from His Holiness. She told me that if I wanted to go to India, she would help me. My parents didn't want to let me go, but I wanted to leave. I cried and pleaded until they agreed.

"My father took me to the road that led to the border, one day's walk away. There we waited until a vehicle came by to take us. We waited for one week next to the road. We slept with people who lived nearby. I was already homesick and at night I had very sad dreams, but it was too late to turn back. My father had arranged everything. At the border the children were all put outside the car. We pretended to be playing and then ran to the other side. It was no problem at all to reach Nepal; my father got through too. He is a salesman and therefore has a passport.

"In Nepal he took me to the reception center. They took pictures of us and then he left. He told me, 'Study hard, listen to your teachers and take care that you get your blessing. After that I'll come and get you.' So we were put on a bus to Delhi and then to Dharamsala. The audience with His Holiness was like a dream. For us, the Dalai Lama is the Buddha of Compassion. In Tibet, when we were small, we felt rich if we had a picture of him. We would be really proud and show everybody. My parents told me about Tibet's religious sides, and that His Holiness lived in India. I didn't learn about the political problems until I came here.

"In Dharamsala I was enrolled in the Tibetan Children's Village School. I studied English and Tibetan. My Tibetan was very good, my father had taught me many prayers and the lessons in our village school were all in Tibetan. We had a good teacher there, a monk, and when I came here I knew no Chinese at all. I could only count to a hundred.

"In the beginning I was very lonely. This was such a strange place, with all this forest. We were used to vast empty spaces. I tried to get over my homesickness by studying hard. We all started in the 'Opportunity Class' and from there on they would decide where you would go next. I was one of the best, I became class president and editor of the school paper. I was planning to become a journalist; that way I would be able to write about Tibet. But I also had to think about my family in Tibet. It would be risky if I started publishing articles against the Communist Party. So in the end I became a doctor.

"Here I studied Tibetan medicine and astrology, plus physics and English. A Tibetan doctor has to know astrology, it's very important for a diagnosis. There is a relationship between the inner elements and the seasons outside. Some medicines also have to be produced on a certain day to have their optimal strength.

"We diagnose an illness by looking at the elements: water, fire, wood and iron. We base the science of death on these points too. As soon as the elements start to mingle, someone's health deteriorates. Wait, let me read it to you: 'When earth mingles with water, the patient becomes blind. When water mixes with fire, the skin becomes dry. When fire blends with wind, the body loses its temperature, and finally, if wind combines with air, the body will stop breathing.' What I'm reading here is a text that was written 3,500 years ago. In those days doctors were mostly monks and there were few books. Nowadays everybody can study them.

"We start a consultation by feeling someone's pulse. If the heart beats quickly, it means that the fire and wind element is strong. A slow pulse means that there is more earth and water. Every element has a connection to a body part: fire goes with the heart and intestines, earth with the stomach, iron with the lungs, and so on. We can feel 12 different pulses, six for warm illnesses and six for cold ones. A warm illness is an infection, anything with a fever, and a cold sickness is for example diabetes and rheumatism. People suffering from those different diseases all have different pulses. We also look at the whole person and we ask many questions, then we check the urine; the color and the bubbles give information about the person's health. When looking at bubbles you must check how long it takes for them to pop.

"We have all kinds of herbs to cure problems. Some medicines warm up and others cool down. I think that they're effective in about 75 percent of cases. They work really well for chronic illnesses like rheumatism. We also have calming herbs for patients with mental problems.

"We now run 40 clinics in this area; most of our patients are Indians. We treat the poor for free, and students and monks also don't pay. Government officials have to pay, but they get priority. They serve the community, so they should go back to work as soon as possible. Other people pay for consultations, but the costs are so low that it doesn't really cover our expenses. In the end it's the community that pays for us.

"I think I'll always stay here. When I started to study Tibetan medicine, I soon became fascinated, and in any case we can't go back to Tibet; too many political problems there. The Chinese say that the Tibetan medicine is Chinese. Of course there are similarities, but the two sciences developed independently of each other.

"Our clinics are very small, but we do our best to expand. We have to fight the big Western pharmaceutical companies, as they work against us. If our form of medicine becomes successful, it would be very bad for them. But even in the West there is more interest; we get more Western patients. Most of them are travelers who have fallen ill with diarrhea or food poisoning. Some have psychological problems, most of the time because of a relationship issue like a divorce. We also get Western cancer patients who come looking for a cure. Our herbs are very good for cancer. They won't cure the illness, but they can prolong life. I once had a patient who was supposed to die within six weeks. I heard that they lived for another four years because of our medicines. We don't know how to cure AIDS. Some of these patients have tried out our herbs and they said that they helped, but I can't say this for sure. After all, I'm just a normal doctor. I can't perform miracles."

11.

SUPERMARKET BUDDHISTS

Some time ago I found a Spanish beauty in a restaurant here, sobbing into a plate of chicken heads. I understood immediately, as the food around here is certainly something to cry about. So I was surprised to hear that the chicken heads were not the cause of her distress. Maria is a member of a big group of world travelers who suffer from a big heart. One fateful day, she felt sorry for the children in the street and decided single-handedly to lift them out of their misery. Maria pulled a Rimpoche, or living Buddha, off the street and together they started an orphanage. Twenty-two children were taken in and housed in a dwelling that belonged to the living Buddha. Maria paid for the reconstruction, furnishings and the running costs of the orphanage. She signed a contract to do so for the next 12 years. You can see it coming; the Rimpoche (I call him the Ruinshilla) was overjoyed and was laughing his head off. Maria is paying though the nose, the kids are grossly neglected and, as if that wasn't enough, Maria has been refused entry to her own orphanage.

Maria begged me for help. I told her to go talk to a Tibetan organization or authority and of course she ran straight to the Tibetan Red Cross (why didn't I keep my mouth shut?) where the other staff members immediately thought that it was a great idea. The Red Cross went to have a look and now wants to take over the care of the children. Attempts to reconcile Maria and the Buddha gave no results. You'd better talk to a yak; the chance of getting hurt from that encounter is much smaller. The man is terribly aggressive. As far as I'm concerned, he can start his trip back to heaven today.

So now what? The Red Cross delegation did identify all kinds of problems with taking over the orphanage. We're sure we can get the Ruinshilla back on the cobblestones of Lhasa, but what do we do after that? Maybe Maria can help out after all. She'll be delighted, and I'm sure she'll immediately go on to create a new problem. I will bet a herd of yaks that she will soon be in business again with the next money-seeking Tibetan. In the meantime, the kids are the real victims of all this. They are so dirty, it hurts to look at them and once again they are hungry. It's heartbreaking.

(From the newsletter of Tineke Ceelen, Lhasa)

Flying saucers? Of course there are flying saucers! I have seen many, both in the sky and on the ground, and I have even been for a trip in one. Tibet is the most convenient country of all for flying saucers. It is remote from the bustle of the everyday world, and is peopled by those who place religion and scientific concepts before material gain. Throughout the centuries, the people of Tibet have known the truth about flying saucers, what they are, why they are, how they work, and the purpose behind it all. We know of the flying saucer people as the gods in the sky in their fiery chariots.

(Tuesday Lobsang Rampa, 'Home of the Gods' in *My Visit to Venus*)

Over the years, Tibet has inspired vivid fantasies in many foreigners. The high, isolated mountain landscape, inhabited by piteous Buddhist monks, was virtually unknown until Austrian mountaineer Heinrich Harrer discovered it in the 1930s. It's no wonder people liked to make up stories about this land. Where else will you find colorful dances performed by monks, a welcoming singing population, mysterious writing in strange characters and golden Buddha statues, and all this on a high mountain plateau in the most isolated part of the world? It's not the political conflicts that attract tourists to Tibet, but the mysterious culture. Heinrich Harrer talks in his second book *Return to Tibet* about the lure of the region. "It was a mysterious country," he writes. "A population that no one had seen, with big and mysterious monasteries, hidden far behind the snowy mountains. You could express everything there, all dreams and desires. You heard about monks who were able to levitate and who could separate their spirits from their bodies. Very few visitors were able to describe this country, and the few individuals who had managed to go were tempted to invent fantastic stories."

One of these fantasy writers is the Lobsang, the flying saucer man. In his book, Harrer destroys the reputation of the famous author. "During my trip through England, where I was giving a series of lectures, my publisher told me that there was now a sensational book about Tibet. My friend Frederick Warburg, the publisher, sent us prints so we could see for ourselves. After I had skimmed the texts, I knew immediately that this man was a swindler. It was the book by Lobsang Rampa, who stated that he had lived in Lhasa and worked as a doctor, during the same time as I had been there. ... In the end Marco Pallis, a Tibetan scholar and Buddhist, decided to track the writer down. He engaged a detective who pretended to be a follower of Lobsang Rampa. He found out that even members of the British aristocracy came to meditate with this man. He had a long, wavy beard and sat surrounded by Siamese cats on a high bed. But in fact he was the son of a plumber from Wales, who first had a car accident, then went around the country as a traveling salesman and had found out that he could make people believe anything if he was clever enough. So he became a fortune teller."

Despite criticism from Tibet experts all over the world, the British salesman went on to publish 13 books and even now, after his death, has a huge following. One web article about his hoax invited the following comment from one of Rampa's followers: "Your review on TL Rampa is rather outdated and is borne out of an incredible constipated realization of truth. I have studied his works for the last 25 years and boy are you WRONG! But then you have no knowledge of transmigration and the higher dimensions that pervade all universes. Learn to see within yourself first before you write such drivel. The ultimate HOAX is you, as you believe in your limited 2D reality. If you practiced one iota of TLR's techniques, you would see the truth for yourself instead of begging (for hoaxes). But then idiots like yourself are what make the web fun, I suppose. So dream on."

The Tibetans themselves are also not very happy with all the fantasy tales about their country. The Dalai Lama, in his autobiography, dismisses the doctor. "Many Westerners want to know whether the books on Tibet by people like Lobsang Rampa and some others, in which they speak about occult practices, are true. They also ask whether Shambala (a legendary country referred to by certain scriptures and supposed to lie among the northern wastes of Tibet) really exists. In reply to the first two questions, I usually say that most of these books are works of imagination and that Shambala exists, yes, but not in a conventional sense."

The lure of Tibet, however, is stronger than ever. Even though tourists can now visit the monasteries themselves and are no longer dependent on the stories of conmen, they still see many things in Tibet that aren't really there. Tibet just can't get rid of its myths. The hard reality of a country in poverty and political turmoil doesn't seem to reach those who come looking for enlightenment.

As a visitor who is not looking for spirituality, I find the temples in Tibet dirty, dark and depressing. Even the Potala, the Dalai Lama's old palace, is like a castle from the middle ages. I find it hard to imagine how anyone could stand living there. Tibet, for me, is a country that is stuck in a complicated political problem. But many Westerners are so taken by the Tibetan mysteries, the mountains and the friendly people, that they only see Buddhas. Much has to do with expectations; Tibet looks beautiful on TV, so the tourists come looking for inspiration or, as one tourist put it, "to work on my karma."

Tineke Ceelen takes me to a few restaurants in Lhasa that are frequented by foreigners – places where the Western seekers of mysticism meet each other. They're hard to find during the winter months, when Tineke spends time with the few aid workers who stay behind. But as soon as the tourist season starts, the capital is filled with seeking souls. They're not very approachable, though. That night we meet a young American man. He's been in Tibet for ten years and goes from one job to the next. Everything is fine, as long as he gets to stay. But he refuses to speak to journalists.

The Western Buddhists do know where to find Tineke. "I'm one of the few foreigners who lives here the whole year round, so whenever they need anything, they come to me," she says. "One day, a group of women walked into my office to announce that the world was about to come to an end. I hadn't even had breakfast yet. But it turned out that we were going to be fine, because only Tibet was going to continue to exist. Another day we had this guy who wore a giant crucifix on his chest. We immediately gave him the nickname Chris Cross. He was writing a book about spiritual enlightenment, and now needed a permit to spend a year in meditation in a cave not far from here. But the Public Security Bureau refused to give permission. He asked if we could help him. In exchange he would teach us meditation techniques that we could use to cure illnesses." Tineke calls the Westerners who visit her 'supermarket Buddhists'. "They take what they want from the shelves and leave the rest."

Many of the lost souls who flock to Tibet think that spirituality is found in the mountains instead of in themselves. The visits sometimes end tragically. There is the story of the American woman who jumped off a cliff because she thought she could fly. She ended up seriously wounded in hospital. Another wanted to join a monastery. When she was refused, she totally lost her mind; she ran around the streets naked and hit the doctors who were trying to help her. The local authorities didn't want to take responsibility for her, as it wasn't clear who would pay for her treatment. In the end, staff of the consulate had to come and repatriate her. It turned out that the woman had a past of psychological problems. When she reached Lhasa, she thought that the spiritual level of the country would keep her stable, so she stopped taking her medication.

When I attended secondary school in Holland, I had a social studies teacher who was a follower of Maharishi Yogi, an Indian meditation guru with the usual long white beard. The guru could levitate and walk through walls. My teacher told us that, through meditation, he had been able to go back to his former lives. He saw how he had been a simple monk. In this life he was a teacher in a small Dutch town, so I'm not sure whether he was making much progress from one life to the next. He taught us meditation techniques which were good for finding some tranquility. I still use the techniques sometimes when I can't sleep. But when I tell the monks in the Jokhang temple about my teacher's abilities, they start giggling. "Maybe he can come here and teach us something, because we don't know how to see our former lives," they say.

My teacher was a very mellow follower compared to Buddhists of this century. There are centers for Tibetan Buddhism all over the world and Westerners can become monks there. The Buddhist way of life is especially popular in the higher classes, and the numbers are growing spectacularly. When the Dalai Lama visited Australia in 1982, there were 35,000 Buddhists in the country. The religious leader gave some low-key lectures at universities. In 1996, during his second visit, 140,000 followers received him. The media dubbed the visit "the Dalai Lama show." The trip was sponsored by Nike and Ford, and admission tickets for a three-day meditation session cost about two hundred dollars. They were sold out weeks in advance.

The Eastern religion is also popular in Hollywood. The most famous Buddhist movie star is Richard Gere, who even got married the Tibetan way. Gere often meets the Dalai Lama and he also goes on retreats to Tibet to get back in touch with his Buddhist self. According to Gere, he spends his time in Tibet in a simple room and has to share a bathroom. He has, while there, a limited supply of water and no television, air conditioning or newspapers. Gere calls this his time to relax, to meditate and to release. Other famous Buddhists include Orlando Bloom, Beastie Boy Adam Yauch and Kate Bosworth.

Westerners who want to study Buddhism have a much easier time than the Tibetan monks. If you type 'Tibetan Buddhism' into your search engine, you'll get an endless list of Western institutions: Chenrezig Tibetan Buddhist Center of Philadelphia; Kurukulla Center for Tibetan Buddhist Studies ("offers courses in Buddhism and meditation, community events and chanting ceremonies. Everyone welcome. Friendly environment"); Ewam Choden Tibetan Buddhist Center in Kensington, California; Kagyu Samye Dzong London ("Tibetan Buddhist Centre opened in April 1998, provides peace and tranquility for all at its two centres in central London") are just the first few.

Not all Westerners who study Buddhism exaggerate. The Dutch meditation teacher in the next interview is a serious practitioner who also talks about the difficulties his teacher had with Western followers. Han de Wit starts his interview by saying that he has never been to Lhasa or India. He understood early enough that spirituality is not found in dark temples or cold mountains.

Western followers of the Dalai Lama also flock to Dharamsala. While I'm eating in a restaurant with Karma, the guide from the Information Department, a blonde girl walks by, one of many. She has short hair, wears a filthy T-shirt and on top of that a seemingly endless Indian sari. Unlike the Tibetans, the Westerners are terribly rude, especially to someone like me, a visitor who does not walk around wearing batik. Everybody's favorite is a small Western boy of about ten years old who is already a monk. During the day, the little boy in robes plays with the Tibetans in the temple of the Dalai Lama.

Karma had to laugh in his usual friendly way. "His Holiness has already suggested that he doesn't encourage Western people to convert to his religion, but they just keep on coming." He's right. In his autobiography, the Dalai Lama writes: "I am always glad if someone derives benefit from adopting Buddhist practices. However, when it actually comes to people changing their religion, I usually advise them to think the matter through very carefully. Rushing into a new religion can give rise to mental conflict and is nearly always difficult."

The Dalai Lama has religious followers enough to deal with. What he is looking for in the West is political support.

HAN DE WIT, THE WESTERN BUDDHIST

Han F. de Wit is a Buddhist meditation teacher and writer of a series of books about Buddhism in the West. After all my travels around China, Tibet and India, it's strange to talk about Buddhism with a nondescript Western man who lives in a typical tiny brick house in a drizzly Dutch town. "I'm a Buddhist, but I've never been to India or Tibet. I studied in the United States," he says.

"In the year seven AD there was a prediction that said when there were birds made of iron and iron horses, the Dharma would move to the West. Those iron birds are airplanes, and the horses are cars, so Buddhism is coming.

"I'm a research psychologist, and as a meditation teacher I work for the Shambhala centers, where we practice Vajrayana Buddhism. Here they call it Tibetan Buddhism, but in fact it originates in India. After that it spread to Tibet and got its own character, but you can still find the Indian influences too.

"I studied psychology in Groningen and later in Amsterdam. My major was methodology; how you set up research. When I was studying, I noticed that there are many subjects not covered in the field of psychology. If you look at a glossary of a psychology book, you won't find words like love, wisdom, doubt or suffering. There is a whole dimension that is ignored, while all these terms have a relation to the psyche. So I started looking around for publications that did talk about these issues. The easiest to find were the women's magazines and the works of some philosophers. The thing these two have in common is that scientific psychologists don't take them seriously. Then I found out that you could also find this terminology in religious traditions, and mostly on the spiritual side of the religion, the practicing part of it. That's where people think about questions like, 'What do you do with fear, with short-sightedness? How can you become a wiser and more generous person?' The answers to these kinds of questions tell us about our spirit and our way of life. They form their own kind of psychology. I called this Contemplative Psychology and wrote about it in my books.

"That brought me to Buddhism. This tradition is so interesting because it has such an expansive contemplative psychology. It's a religion in which the human being is the focal point. There isn't really a god in Buddhism. It's a philosophy, not a religion. It's also very practical. Western religions are very conceptual, it's very important to know the theory, the catechism. But there's hardly any religious practice left in the West. Who still spends half an hour a day praying? Praying is a form of practice and it is important; it puts you into contact with your spirit. Buddhism gives you an array of exercises that help you get a lucid spirit and feel compassion. It also has an interesting way of thinking about ethics. In the West, there is a tendency to put ethics into laws of what is allowed and what isn't; the laws of society or the church. Buddhism also has some prohibitions, but they are not laws. They only serve to open your heart so you can live a caring and faithful life.

"Apart from my psychological interest in Buddhism I also had a personal reason that brought me to this spiritual tradition, 35 years ago now. At that time, I was a successful student and I thought that science was the most valuable thing that Western culture had to offer. I already published during my studies, then graduated *cum laude*. But because of that, I started wondering, 'Is this what life is all about?' All this success didn't taste as good as I had hoped. So that's another reason I started to look around. I went to bookshops where a scientist like me normally wouldn't be seen, those small spiritual stores. There I bought a book by a Tibetan Buddhist named Chogyam Trungpa, who later became one of the most famous Vajrayana masters in the West. That book was called *Cutting Through Spiritual Materialism*. I took it with me on a trip to Germany, where I went to visit a center of the Hindu tradition. That center was led by a group of yoginis, young Indian women with beautiful brown eyes and minute faces, all dressed in white. I loved it there. They gave us instructions and we started meditating. After the meditation they asked if we had seen Brahma and I seemed to be the only one who hadn't seen anything.

"On the way back, I took out Chogyam Trungpa's book and started reading. The first chapter was exactly about the attitude with which I had traveled to the center; about the hope that the spiritual path would free me of the is-this-everything-there-is-to-life feeling. Besides that, spirituality is also a kind of exciting entertainment to many people. Trungpa's book talked about Westerners who thought that all would be well as long as they went to spiritual places. But that is just a form of running away from reality, and fleeing has nothing to do with Buddhism. On the contrary, Buddhism is about accepting life, and learning from reality.

"I wrote to Trungpa Rinpoche and went to America. I lived there for two years. In 1976 I took refuge in the three jewels, the ceremony that makes you a Buddhist. In Holland people never have a problem with me being converted. They will say, 'Oh, interesting,' when I tell them. We are a multicultural society. In 1977 I set up a Buddhist center in Amsterdam. That was still Dharma in the living room; I worked from my own house. Later on this became too small and we started a bigger institution, now called the Shambhala Centrum Amsterdam. The building is funded by contributions from members and tuition fees for the courses that we give.

"I meditate every day. Well, sometimes I skip a day, but it's a lot like playing the piano; it's best to practice every day. Sometimes there are meditation sessions that last the whole day, or even longer. In 1977 Chogyam Trungpa gave his permission for me to teach, and since that time I have given courses and lectures.

"When you're a Buddhist, you have a different relationship with the reality of existence. You learn to accept that illness, old age, death, not getting what you want – and getting what you don't want – are all part of life. People who are afraid of death, for example, are scared of the pain and fear that they'll feel when dying. They hope that they can conquer their fear and that it will then go away. But in the Buddhist vision, conquering fear does not mean making it disappear; it means facing it bravely and dealing with it. You also don't think that illness is a mistake of nature; even the Buddha dies.

"When you leave your fear of life and death behind, you can live with more dedication. You learn how to improve a situation. That's different from using a situation to your advantage. We call this concept 'egoless living'.

"Chogyam had a big influence on both Tibetan and Western modern Buddhism. He and his followers managed to translate Buddhism in such a way that it became understandable for Westerners. That gave a big push for Buddhism in the West.

"Chogyam Trungpa started off as the highest lama of his monastery. He fled Tibet when the Chinese started to oppress Buddhism. He traveled over the mountains with three hundred people and went to work for the Dalai Lama in India for a while. He went on to study psychology and philosophy in England, because he wanted to get to know Western culture as much as possible.

"In Scotland he started the first Tibetan Buddhist center in the West. But soon he noticed that the appearance of Buddhism stood between him and his followers. He saw that his Western students were more interested in his robe, citing Tibetan mantras and the sound of Tibetan bells and gongs than in what he had to say. He noticed that he couldn't get through to his students.

"This is why he asked the Dalai Lama for permission to stop being a monk and to start living as a Westerner. This was during the hippie era, so living like a Westerner included having girlfriends, drinking, smoking and partying. This behavior shocked the Tibetan world. Chogyam's own spiritual leaders thought that he had lost all perspective. His Western students also didn't want to accept him in jeans and a sweater, so there was a big conflict.

"In the meantime, he had also got some students in the US, and they invited him to go there. In America he started all over again. He managed to find students who were open to the contents of Buddhism as opposed to looking blindly at the outside forms. Although these American hippies saw him as one of them, they slowly understood that he was a very unique person and that his way of living was that of a real bodhisattva.

"Gradually, the Tibetans also started to accept his way. They saw that his Western followers were really practicing the Dharma. That hadn't happened before. Those first pupils in England were not ready to meditate for hours. They preferred to travel to Nepal and walk around a stupa. The first lamas who had traveled to the West often looked down on Westerners; the lamas didn't understand them and they didn't empathize with them either. The religious leaders knew that they had something valuable to offer, but they saw their Western students as animals in human skin, people who were obsessed by their materialistic passions. They wondered how they could ever teach these people the Dharma. Sometimes they tried to scare them a little with stories about hot and cold hells in which you would end up if you didn't lead a good life.

"It was difficult to have a relationship with Westerners because these people were looking for gurus that they could blindly follow, leaders who would promise them all kinds of things. We still see that a lot, people who are looking for a religion that guarantees that if you follow it, all will be well in life. People have seen a movie about the Dalai Lama or about Asian gurus and they think that to be spiritual, they have to behave like them. For these people, Buddhism is the wrong philosophy. The teachers asked themselves how they could break though this well-meant naivety. They attach very different emotions to their behavior than Westerners do. The Westerners still have to go though a whole process.

"In Buddhism, the relationship between student and teacher is very important. There has to be trust, not a blind following. A good teacher will criticize a student who doesn't think for himself. Only if there is a connection can the Dharma be carried over to the next generation. Because Chogyam Trungpa had this bond with his students, he was able to go a step further; he could educate Westerners so that they could become teachers. He said, 'You don't need to have Asian eyes to be able to teach the Dharma.' So now Westerners are able to pass it on. That was another shock for the Tibetans at that time, but now there is more widespread training of Western teachers. The life story of this Tibetan Dharma teacher is the tale of the ugly duckling that became a swan. After working in the West for some years, Chogyam Trungpa was completely rehabilitated into the Tibetan Buddhist community. After his death, his son, Sakyong Mipham Rinpoche, became the leader of Shambhala

International, an organization that has meditation centers all over the world.

"Nowadays it's easier to deal with these issues. A whole new generation has grown up in Dharamsala. These young people know that you can be Westernized and not lose the core of Buddhism. After all, Buddhism came from India and then went to Tibet, to a completely different culture. It's a transcultural religion, and maybe the West will one day bring it back to Tibet. We can already see this happening. Even before the invasion of the Chinese, Buddhism had lost some of its spiritual force. Teachers traveled around and earned money for performing rituals and ceremonies. The form was still there, but the content, the meaning, wasn't very clear any more. In the end religion is the work of people, and there are always people who hold on too long to the form, thinking that content will come with it. But in other times and cultures, you need to find other forms.

"During the Cultural Revolution, the Chinese fought Buddhism and its teachers and they were very successful. They have robbed the Tibetans of something they considered their most valuable treasure for centuries: a spiritual tradition that tries to cultivate clarity and compassion. Nowadays, the Tibetans are losing these traditions. One of Chogyam Trungpa's students once went back to the monastery of his teacher and he discovered that there were many rituals that the monks there didn't know any more. Some Tibetans believe that if Buddhism had been stronger, the people would have been able to resist the Chinese invaders more strongly."

12.

Democracy in exile

A signed article by Yi Duo on Friday provided an insight into the autocratic nature of the Dalai Lama's theocratic rule. The article said the Dalai clique had been using every opportunity to talk about its democratic achievements for years, while some Western forces have also been trying to portray the Dalai Lama as the symbol of democracy. The article said anyone who knows the Dalai clique would be able to tell that it is an autocratic theocracy that is anything but democratic. The article said the Dalai clique had tried to set a legal basis for its rule. Although it borrowed such concepts as "separation of executive, legislative and judicial powers" from the West, it is still a theocratic system with the Dalai Lama acting as both the head of the government and the religious leader – a system continued from the old Tibet. ...

The article said the Dalai clique is a theocratic regime run by prominent monks. Political favoritism and nepotism is widespread. ... According to their election rules, 10 of the 43 members of the Tibetan Parliament-in-exile must come from different sects of Tibetan Buddhism. The article says the Dalai clique still represents the interests of remnant forces of the feudal serf owners in old Tibet. All the brothers and sisters of the Dalai Lama served in high positions in the Dalai clique. His late eldest brother Taktser Rinpoche used to lead the New York and Japan offices of the "Tibetan government-

in-exile". His wife and three children are now living in the US. The Dalai's second eldest brother Gyalo Thondup, the second most powerful person in the Dalai clique, had held the post of Chief Kalon several times. ... Since the founding of the "Tibetan government-in-exile", seven family members of the Dalai had held the posts of Kalon and Chief Kalon, the article says. "The 14th Dalai Lama's family is much more powerful than the families of all the previous Dalai Lamas."

In addition, a number of powerful people in the "Tibetan government-in-exile" are from old Tibetan nobility or families of old tribal chiefs. Yi's article claims that in order to secure its autocratic rule, the Dalai clique even resort to assassination and poisoning to persecute political and religious dissidents. In the 1990s, the Dalai clique suddenly began attacking the Tibetan deity Dorje Shugden, who had been worshiped by Tibetan Buddhists for hundreds of years, calling it a "pro-Chinese demon". On June 6, 1996, the "Tibetan government-in-exile" adopted a resolution prohibiting all staff of the "Tibetan government-in-exile" as well as all Tibetan communities, lamaseries and schools from worshiping the Dorje Shugden, saying that those who would not stop following the deity would be labeled as public enemies of the Tibetan society.

Yi's article said the Dalai Lama's demonstrations of democracy were done for show. For instance, the Tibetans in exile were even allowed to set up a Tibetan Communist Party and run a number of unofficial newspapers as part of the Dalai Lama's democratic test in the 1960s. But once those organizations and newspapers hurt the interests of the old Tibetan aristocrats in exile, they were threatened and asked to shut down. As a result, the organizations and newspapers quickly disappeared.

(From: Autocratic nature of Dalai clique's theocracy, *China Daily*, Beijing, 2008)

Democracy is something that His Holiness the Dalai Lama has dreamed of giving to his people since he was young. Even before the tragic flight of His Holiness the Dalai Lama and some 80,000 Tibetans into exile in 1959, after the Tibetan National Uprising was crushed by the Chinese, His Holiness the Dalai Lama had introduced several reforms aimed at establishing greater democracy, but his efforts were hampered by the Chinese occupying forces.

(From the Government of Tibet in Exile, Dharamsala)

It's hard to imagine the English-speaking, modern bureaucrats who represent the government-in-exile in Dharamsala as a bunch of medieval slave-owners, even if the Chinese keep depicting them as such. They don't even look aristocratic. Of course, none of the officials in the government ever owned any serfs. They are young, well educated intellectuals who were often born in exile or who fled their homeland at a very young age. In India they created a new society that is the opposite of the system in the old Tibet.

The Dalai Lama himself was the driving force behind the creation of this new mini-country. He used the flight to India as a chance to start the reforms that he had planned in Tibet. In his autobiography he describes how difficult it was to carry out his ideas, as his teachers made all the decisions until the Dalai Lama was old enough. By the time he finally had the right to decide, Tibet was full of Chinese and he had to escape. In India he saw his chance to start all over, with a new society and a new political system. In his youth, the leader writes, he had been interested in Marxism, but in the end decided to settle on a Western democratic system. That is why there is now a parliament-in-exile in the small mountain town.

It's an interesting situation. The religious leader has to deal with followers who will do whatever he orders. They are very happy to just carry out his ideas. Nonetheless, he has managed to get them to be enthusiastic about democratic reforms. Not only is there a parliament; every association or institute is busy holding elections, discussions and workshops. The former colonial summer retreat has become a huge debating camp. All of this is because the Dalai Lama wants it. Were he to decide tomorrow that it's better to install a dictatorship, then that would be fine with the Tibetans, as long as he stays on as leader. As a result, there is one problem with the Tibetan democracy: there isn't really an opposition. Even the radical Youth Congress calls itself "loyal opposition." It disputes the Middle Path, but not the leadership.

There is one group of Tibetan Buddhists who have a religious difference with the Dalai Lama. These are the followers of Dorje Shugden, an ancient deity whom the Lama has branded an evil spirit. Dorje's followers call the religious leader a fundamentalist who uses his religion for political gain. "In recent years, the Dalai Lama has woven a web of deception to maintain his political grip on the Tibetans in exile and bolster his position as a global celebrity commanding millions of dollars in speaking fees and enjoying the adulation of heads of state, Hollywood stars, and other celebrities worldwide," the Dorje Shugden website states.

You can't find Dalai Lama dissidents in Dharamsala. The only time the Tibetans didn't agree with the ideas of their leader was when he wanted to adopt a new law giving the parliament the power to depose him as a political ruler. The people protested and the law wasn't passed; that's democracy after all. So the religious leader is for the time being stuck with his political role, although he constantly warns his followers that he won't be doing this forever. The Dalai Lama is now in his seventies and wishes to retire.

The most important discussions among all the groups in Dharamsala are about ways to approach China. The majority of the followers seem to agree that most hope lies in educating the Chinese so that they will understand what is bad about their colonialist behavior and will ask their leaders to change their policy towards Tibet.

But the exiles disagree on the best way to get China's attention. Members of the Youth Congress are becoming more radical as time goes by. In the past they organized hunger strikes. One was held in front of the United Nations building in Delhi, asking the international organization to hold a special meeting on Tibet. When the hunger strikers didn't get enough support, one of them set himself on fire and died two days later from his wounds. The action set a dangerous precedent. A month later, a French man torched himself because his government had refused to meet the Dalai Lama.

The officials of the government follow a much milder path. The bureaucrat I interviewed stated that the exiles are not allowed to organize radical protests, as they have to abide by Indian law. India granted the Tibetans asylum for humanitarian reasons, but it also made it very clear that it didn't want its territory to be used for anti-Chinese activities.

So the government officials-in-exile have a different task; they try to negotiate with Beijing. Talks on a solution for Tibet and a return of the Dalai Lama started in the 1980s. Deng Xiaoping promised that all issues were negotiable as long as no one spoke about independence. The first talks brought progress in some areas. Family visits between Tibetans in Tibet and those in India became possible and the brother of the Dalai Lama got permission to travel to the region. The Chinese wanted to show how they had brought economic development and religious freedom. In his autobiography, the Dalai Lama writes that he was amazed at their optimism. The Chinese leaders apparently really believed that the Tibetans led happy lives, and this was barely ten years after the atrocities of the Cultural Revolution. The visit by the Dalai Lama's representatives ended in complete humiliation for the Chinese. The brother was overwhelmed by his people, who begged him to help them. After four of these kinds of fact-finding missions, the Chinese had had enough. A plan to send Indian-trained teachers to Tibet was refused.

The negotiations have never stopped, even if there have been no more results. Both sides always declare that they are ready to hold talks without any preconditions, and then immediately start making up stipulations. The Chinese want the Dalai Lama to accept that Tibet is a historical part of China, and he has to stop asking for independence. The Dalai Lama, on the other hand, has spent the last 30 years looking for a workable compromise. In 1987 he wrote a peace plan as a basis for further negotiations, called the Middle Path. It states that while waiting for complete independence, Tibet could be an autonomous region for a while. China would take care of Tibet's foreign affairs and military defense and the Dalai Lama would go back as a religious leader. The internal affairs of the Tibetans would be managed by a democratically elected parliament.

For that to happen, the Dalai Lama wants Tibet to be demilitarized, so that the area could become a peaceful zone between China and India. He also wants China to stop filling the region with Chinese laborers and his last condition stipulates that as soon as he is back in Tibet and the parliament is installed, the Chinese would have to start serious negotiations about independence. The religious leader makes it clear that he refuses to go back if the situation in Tibet doesn't change. He has also stated that he will not endorse any Chinese historical claim on Tibet.

The Chinese responded to the Middle Path with their own five-point plan. In it, they ignored accusations about human rights violations, and they didn't talk about environmental protection or military affairs. Instead, the plan was filled with promises to the Dalai Lama. He would keep his status as religious leader and would get to live in a nice house. This is a blatant example of how much misunderstanding there is between the two sides.

And of course there is no trust. Redi, as a forefront of the Chinese authorities, always says that he is not convinced that the Dalai Lama isn't out to get independence after all. "Sometimes he says that he wants autonomy, but then the next day he'll talk about Tibet as an occupied country. His ideas about autonomy are very different from the system we have now, because after all we are an autonomous region already. Behind him, there is a whole clique of politicians who don't want autonomy either. As soon as the Dalai Lama says that he wants to give up his claim to independence, they jump up and say the opposite. If the Dalai Lama would be clearer on the issue, negotiations would be a lot easier."

By now, there have been six rounds of talks. The latest round broke down after the protests of March 2008. American president George W. Bush urged Chinese president Hu Jintao to restart negotiations, but the leader only answered that the Dalai Lama had to stop sabotaging the Olympic Games – another pre-condition added to the long list.

Because of all these failures, the Dalai Lama himself spends much time thinking about alternatives. In 1994 he tried to hold a referendum, asking the Tibetan people what they wanted him to do. The Chinese, of course, refused to let a referendum take place in Tibet itself as, according to them, the majority of the Tibetans there are not against the Chinese presence. To hold the elections secretly would bring forth another round of oppression, so the leader tried to get his people's opinion through secret messages and informal discussions in Dharamsala. When that didn't work, he gathered all the Tibetans in exile for a big meeting in November 2008. The result: Tibetans still want him to follow the Middle Path, even if it seems hopeless.

People talk a lot about the future of the community after the Dalai Lama passes on. It could take 20 years before a new reincarnation would be old enough to lead the people, so it would be a disaster for Dharamsala if the Dalai Lama were to die before there is a solution. Some Tibetans suggest that is what China is waiting for. The community would fall apart and the Chinese would win.

But the Tibetans also warn that if the Chinese want to find a solution, it will be much more complicated without the religious leader. And they are sure that one day there will have to be a compromise. Though there may be no diplomatic recognition of Tibet, the international pressure is growing. Ten years ago there was no state leader willing to receive the Dalai Lama. Last year, the French president and the EU did receive the religious leader, Chinese protests or not.

The unsuccessful actions of the Dalai Lama do have one effect: they keep the more radical youth from starting a violent struggle. Once the religious leader passes away, these impatient youngsters will have no one to hold them back. The Tibetans would never be able to win a war against the Chinese, but the refugees have built up so much frustration that they don't care any more. The negotiating government officials and the members of the Youth Congress agree on one point: Something has to happen. They can't wait another 50 years.

TSETEN NORBU, THE EXTREMIST

"That hunger strike we organized had a big effect. It also woke people up when one of us burned himself. Of course, we didn't tell that man that he should do this, but I think that we shared his frustrations. Nobody wanted to support us at the beginning of our fast, not even our own people. They said, 'You will go into hunger strike and the Dalai Lama will ask you to stop and then you'll listen to him.' But now we've shown the world that we mean what we say, that we will give our lives for Tibet. It was a clear message to all the exiles here. If they really want to be independent they have to pay a price. Next time they will take us seriously."

Tseten Norbu has a thin mustache and a round face. He lives in another of these small houses next to a muddy road in McLeod. Tseten is not very interested in telling his life story. He races through it so he can get to the political part. He talks about his work as loyal opposition. Stirring up a little trouble in the refugee society stimulates democracy, he says. "The Tibetans here are much too obedient."

"I don't know when I was born. At some time at 1959, when I was about three months old, I was given to my grandparents. They lived on the other side of Mount Everest and they took me to Nepal. My parents were nomads and they traded. They were used to traveling up and down between Tibet and Nepal. But one day they didn't come back. I heard that my father died in prison; he had been arrested because of political activities. My younger brother still lives in Tibet. He has five children, none of them go to school, but he doesn't want to go to India. In any case it's too dangerous to escape with five children. And he likes the place where he lives. My mother came to visit me here in 1985 when I was 28 years old. That was the first time I had seen her.

"I grew up in the Tibetan community in exile in Nepal. We were completely dependent on aid money. I remember how we earned money by building houses. It was a kind of food-for-work program. For us children everything was arranged. In 1972, I went to secondary school. All young people were enrolled. All those years that I was growing up there was no communication with my parents or with Tibet. I didn't even know whether they were still alive.

"Life in the community was not easy; I always went to school with an empty stomach. But you did have a reason to be there. The teachers told us daily how they had fought the Chinese and fled over the Himalayas. They told us, 'You are the seeds of Tibet. You have to fight for your country.' That gave us a very nationalistic feeling. These lessons had a very good influence on us. We learned to be frugal and careful. My own children are not like that. They spend so much money on unimportant things. We learned life the hard way. We had to go to school together with the Nepalese. They didn't have any problems and they had everything they needed, so they studied much better than we did. But my life always had a clear goal. As soon as I finished my studies at the university, I went to work for government institutes. First I worked in Katmandu, where there were many new refugees. I also helped to manage a carpet factory.

"We automatically became members of the Youth Congress. We now have 13,000 members and 65 chapters all over the world. My task is to take care that we have a good work program. Every three years we hold a big meeting and we decide what we are going to do. We have always described ourselves as loyal opposition. We try to help the government by giving suggestions and trying to influence them, but we are not a real political party. In 1970 we decided that we would keep on fighting for total independence, despite the concessions of the Dalai Lama.

"We also tried to block the government's referendum. They wanted all the exiles to vote on which line we should follow. There were four choices: independence, the Middle Path of the Dalai Lama, holding on to the truth, or autonomy. Our first criticism was that the differences between these points were not clear. We were not afraid that they would vote against independence. If we find out that nobody wants that, then that's fine, we will stop demanding it. But you can't hold such a referendum. It's impossible to do it inside Tibet and there are only 100,000 refugees on the outside. It would be a historical mistake if we didn't ask the majority of the Tibetans anything and let the minority here decide our policy. So we had an election for or against the referendum and we won. Sixty five percent of the Tibetans agreed with us, so we didn't hold the referendum.

"We believe that we need many different opinions. If you don't, then you can't have democracy. There aren't enough voices in this community. The bureaucrats who work for the government are much too passive. The Dalai Lama told us years ago that we should start many political parties, but those bureaucrats don't do that at all. They don't listen, because it's not to their benefit.

"We also think we have to work on educating the Chinese. A whole generation has grown up in China and they know nothing about the problems in Tibet. That is our most important task, to contact the people there. We also communicate with the Taiwanese, with dissidents abroad and overseas Chinese. They all have families in China and so they can spread our message there. The Tibetans in Lhasa should do the same, talk to their Chinese friends. Nowadays, the information in China is more free and more Chinese writers are interested in Tibet. We have to use that. I also think we should start more projects to help the Tibetans. If we cannot do so directly, we could do it through other organizations.

"I think the government here spends too much time traveling around and talking to the international community. Not one government has supported us until now and as long as they don't, the Chinese won't understand. They only react to real pressure, so we need to convert all that sympathy from the West into real actions by their governments. And if that doesn't happen, we should stop. We can't keep on traveling and asking for help. For every thousand rupees that we spend traveling abroad we should spend at least another thousand on influencing the Chinese people.

"Most of all we think that we need to be more active, not always just reacting to what the Chinese government does and says. You have to make your own movement and your own program. Our hunger strike was a good example. In Tibet people are fighting and they're giving their lives. Now they got a message from us that we want to do something too. If our way of protesting doesn't help, we'll find another one. Within the community the call for tougher actions is becoming louder. There are some small groups in Tibet who have chosen to explode bombs. These are independent groups and we have no connection to them, but we have to think about their ways too. If our protests don't go anywhere, we'll have to decide on our next step. If we wait for another 50 years, independence will be useless, Tibet will be full of Chinese. We have to reach our goal while the Dalai Lama is still alive, and we are running out of time."

SONAM N. DAGPO, THE GOVERNMENT OFFICIAL

"In 1960 we started to buy the land. Until that time the government in exile worked and lived in renovated barns. We thought we didn't have to build houses because we were planning to go back to Tibet soon. So we stayed in those barns for ten years. But in the end there were so many refugees, and it took so much time, that we had to get organized."

Nowadays Sonam works in a modern office in the Information Department. It's an ironic name, because in Beijing all foreign journalists are also the responsibility of an Information Department. The Chinese bureaucrats who work there are professional diplomats who are rotated to Chinese embassies all over the world. They are well educated and helpful. They give out blue work permits and chat with journalists, mostly about their colleagues. It is also their job to lecture naughty foreign reporters. Once in a while they organize trips for the press during which participants don't really learn anything but get to eat a lot of food. The office is located in an enormous building on one of Beijing's boulevards. Their Tibetan counterparts in India have a less spacious workplace, but their distribution of information is ten times more efficient.

"I am from Dagpo, that's why it's my name. At the Tibetan school here we were all given the same last names as the places where we came from. That way we wouldn't forget our hometowns. My parents were rich farmers, the kind the Chinese call slave owners. They owned land and had many yaks. There were people who worked for them as well, but they weren't really slaves. I helped to write *Truth from Facts*, the book we published about the social system in the old Tibet. The society then was not as oppressive as the Chinese want us to believe.

"My parents fled a year after the first revolt. My father was arrested in 1959 and had to stay a year in prison. I was very small and I remember that my uncle took me to visit him. We went by horse, it took about a day. The prison was located in an old monastery. There was a river behind the building and that's where I played with my father. It wasn't a very strict jail. My father introduced me to all the other inmates and told me that I should call them uncles. After he was released, we escaped. I remember sliding down the mountains in the snow. There was no road and the only way to get down was to slide, it was scary. India in 1962 was preparing to go to war with China, so there were many Indian soldiers at the border. They helped us and a lot of other refugees who came at the same time. We were with five children. The soldiers put us in an airplane. Can you imagine? I was four years old, straight from the mountains, and was put on a plane. I got sick and I had to throw up in my mother's lap.

"We ended up in a refugee camp for Tibetans. Every day people died, often because they couldn't stand the climate. My father was afraid that we would get sick too. He refused to stay in that camp with five little children, but you weren't allowed to leave. So he decided to escape again. One night we ran away into the jungle. My uncle came to get us there and took us to India.

"In Darjeeling we had to help build the roads like all the other refugees. We built the infrastructure in the entire area in exchange for food. When I was eight years old, I was allowed to go to school. The Dalai Lama negotiated with the Indian government and they built a school for us here. This is when the school for orphans was also founded. We followed the Indian school system, but we also learned Tibetan and the history of Tibet. Our teachers told us that we had to study hard and spend our lives serving the government. After the roads were all done, we wondered what we should do next. In the end we started to build houses. The Dalai Lama wanted to create a real Tibetan community. We got land from Nehru and that's when we built the first villages here.

"Our ideas about staying here started to change too. We realized that we would be in India for a long time and that we had to do something to save the culture and traditions. We also knew that we couldn't believe the Chinese. The propaganda sometimes said that we could go back to Tibet without any problems, but those were lies. My father knows the methods and lies of the Chinese authorities. He learned about them in prison. They would tell him, 'If you betray the others, we will let you go.' But my father didn't fall for that. The Chinese don't see us as equals. They are the new masters and they think like colonialists. They don't feel any obligation to tell the truth.

"In Delhi I studied history and I wanted to become a teacher. In the eighties the first exchanges between the Dalai Lama and the Chinese government took place. When the Chinese said that young educated people could go to work in Tibet as teachers, it sounded like something for me. But then they started to make up excuses. They said that the facilities in Tibet were not yet up to standard, so that it would be better if we went to a university in China first. In the end nobody got a visa, so I became involved in the negotiations. I didn't go on the missions, but I did a lot of the paperwork. After the fourth delegation had gone to Tibet, the authorities didn't want to let the inspectors in any more. Then His Holiness presented his peace plan in 1987, and they swept that off the table. They also didn't agree with the members of the negotiation team, saying that it couldn't include any officials of the government-in-exile. And they only wanted to negotiate in Beijing, so that was the end of that round.

"In 1993, they said that they were ready to conduct realistic talks again. We sent a delegation to Beijing, but again there was no result. After that we'd had enough. We passed a resolution in the parliament in which we declared that we would not initiate talks any more because they were useless. Only if China or a third country wanted to restart negotiations, would we participate. Later on, we decided to go back to the old ways.

If we don't, nothing happens at all, so now we have more freedom to initiate contact. Not that that changes anything. Every time we meet the Chinese negotiators, they start to lecture us and to complain about our separatist activities.

"Here we work to set up a democratic system. In the past our government was not democratic, the aristocrats held power. The Chinese media constantly say that the Dalai Lama backs the old system, but His Holiness is much more progressive than that. Now we have an elected parliament and a constitution, for the free Tibet of the future. In 1993 we added more democratic reforms. We dissolved the parliament and had direct elections. We also kept some parts of the old system, because in the old Tibet the villagers elected their own heads and we still do that here. We have divided up the camps into villages and so everybody can choose their own leaders.

"When I was at the university I was also president of the Youth Congress, so I understand that those youngsters want tougher actions. Of course they are impatient, but they don't understand that we have our limits as a government. The Indian authorities told His Holiness very clearly that he was not allowed to carry out political activities. This is why he gave his most important speeches outside of India, in Geneva, for example. The Indian government has helped us a lot with building up the community and the cultural institutes, but politics are still sensitive. So we don't call ourselves a government, but an administration. Nowadays the restrictions on political activities are not so tight. In the beginning we were not allowed to demonstrate or wave a Tibetan flag. That has changed. You still need to ask permission to hold protest marches, and if it is refused and you go anyway, you get arrested. When the Chinese leaders visited India, we all went. We stood in front of the Chinese embassy. I was arrested twice and locked up for a week. We sat in prison and joked about the quality of the food. But in fact we had an easier time than those outside who hadn't been arrested. They had to run around trying to get us released.

"Over the last few years the government has given me different posts. That's what my life is like, I work where they send me. Since I was young I always wanted to do this kind of job. We will always continue to be employed like this, until we can go back to Tibet. Even if it lasts five, ten, or one hundred years. We know that as long as we are here, we have to safeguard our heritage. In that we stand united."

13.

THE FORGOTTEN SISTERS

With us neither the one sex nor the other is considered the inferior or the superior. Men and women treat each other as equals. The women are not kept in seclusion, but take full part in social life and in business affairs. Husband and wife are companions and partners, but the husband is the head of the household, and not the wife, as some of your writers have it. The status of women in our country is much the same as in yours. The wife manages the household. She holds the keys and also usually takes charge of the family money and her husband consults her in his affairs. They consult each other, they decide everything together. Grown up sons and daughters are also consulted. The family decides its affairs as a whole. ... So the Tibetan woman from her childhood learns to be useful and self-reliant and capable. She is at ease with men, for she has mixed with them, with her brothers and boys in general, and in equality from the start.

(*We Tibetans*, 1926)

Women were discriminated against as the "lowborn" of humanity in the old Tibet under the feudal-slave system. In the written law of the old local government of Tibet, it is stipulated in explicit terms: "Women have no right to discuss state affairs" and "Slaves and women may not take part in military and state affairs."... In the old

Tibet, people believed women to be witches, demi-demons, unlucky creatures and incarnations of catastrophe. In summer, women were not permitted to shout or play while laboring in the field for fear of causing a natural calamity such as a hailstorm or frost, which would damage the crops. … Since ancient times, Tibet had been paralyzed by such beliefs as "men are born superior and women inferior," and so from infancy boys and girls were differentiated.

(*Tibet, the Land and the People,* Tiley Chodag, New World Press, Beijing)

Just like the Chinese stories keep repeating how cruel landlords in the old Tibet oppressed slaves and the poor, they also try to prove that the situation of women was appalling. The exiled Tibetans in India deny this, but they are not the only ones. There is the account of Rinchen Lhamo of 1926. She came from Kham, was the first Tibetan woman to marry a British man, and moved to London in the 1920s. There she wrote a book, *We Tibetans*. In simple style she described her country at that time, long before the Chinese army invaded it, so her accounts are free of any political standpoint.

Rinchen was offended by all the nonsense the British media wrote about Tibet. She denies rumors that Tibet was a polygamous society, where women could marry more than one man. "Some of your writers say that polyandry obtains as a form of marriage in Tibet. It does not. One writer, who did not go to Kham, and speaks from hearsay only, says it is universal in Kham, that is, from where I myself come. It is not true. I did not know there was such a thing as polyandry until I came amongst you and learned you believed it to be prevalent in our country." Rinchen describes the Tibetans as a traditional people with a pleasantly arranged society, without too many problems. Women know their place.

But, Rinchen observes, they have more to say than their contemporaries in England.

The modern Tibetan women's associations seem to agree. Their own men do not oppress Tibetan women, they say, so the organizations are not interested in feminism. Instead, they only exist to fight against the Chinese oppressors. Once those are gone, all will be well, or so the women believe.

The first Tibetan women that I interview sit, soaking wet from a downpour, in the Press Center in Huairou, the place where non-governmental organizations take part in the International Women's Conference in Beijing. Timidly I ask one of them for her life story. She's an elderly woman who has lived in Canada for 20 years and still doesn't speak any English. She is surrounded by the younger generation, who are fluent and very Westernized. The youngsters were born and studied in the West and became militant freedom fighters.

These women are lucky to be in China at all. Other Tibetan women's groups who wanted to take part in the conference were denied visas. This group presented itself as a normal feminist association and therefore made it through customs. "We are here to speak for the sisters in Tibet, because they are not allowed to say anything," one of them states.

Speaking up may be easy, but being heard is another matter. The Chinese police let them have a demonstration against Chinese occupation, but this has to take place on a designated soccer field. As many women had expressed the desire to march, the Chinese, who don't want trouble in Huairou, find a field with lots of space and no listeners. The Tibetan women also try to give workshops on the situation in Tibet, but these get disturbed by both Chinese and Tibetans working for the government, they complain. The Tibetan cadres are also represented at the conference. They have a beautifully embroidered tent right next to the entrance, while it's hard to even find the exiles. "The Chinese are trying to cause problems between us and the official Tibetan women," one of the young translators complains.

That doesn't seem to be very difficult, because the translator herself starts arguing with anybody who dares even look at us. It's almost impossible to get the old woman's story straight because of all the interruptions. "Wait first," the translator exclaims. "That woman over there is listening to us." And then, in an aggressive tone to a woman who is, indeed, curiously listening in: "Excuse me, who are you? We're having a private conversation here!" The woman starts to smile bashfully. "I'm Tibetan," she answers. "Chinese-Tibetan."

She's not the only one who gets sent away. Even the Chinese who are selling arts and crafts behind a table, and are peacefully reading the newspaper, are potential spies. "They eavesdrop all the time and try to take our picture," the translator complains. "We have a bodyguard network. We never go anywhere by ourselves, but we move around in a group. That way the Chinese can't arrest us." I suggest that the Chinese wouldn't do that, because these women have foreign passports and arresting them would create an international scandal. The translator looks at me suspiciously. Unlike the translator, the old woman does want to communicate with the Chinese-Tibetans. "You shouldn't blame them," she tells her friend softly. "They don't have a choice." Even though she's the only one in the group who was actually oppressed by the Chinese, she seems to have a much milder opinion. "The Chinese party leaders have a nice life, but the rest of the population here also lives under a dictatorship, just like the Tibetans," she says.

The woman's story is mostly about her husband, who got in trouble right after China's invasion. He fled in 1958, a year before the Dalai Lama left for India. "Life wasn't perfect before the Chinese came, but it was peaceful and without difficulties," she remembers. "When the Chinese soldiers came, we welcomed them. The first years that they were there weren't so bad. The soldiers were very friendly. They told us they had come to help us and then they would leave again. They started to build schools and hospitals. The Tibetans were so gullible; they really thought that the Chinese only wanted to help. They became friends with the soldiers."

The woman's husband was one of the first who distrusted the newcomers. "He formed a group of 40 people. They would meet at our house and make up a strategy against the Chinese." The result was that they started to feel the hand of oppression right away. "The Chinese would come and disturb the meetings, and there were infiltrators. Soon we had to keep the meetings in secret. When the Chinese found out, they arrested three leaders. My husband tried to help his friends in jail. Every day he brought them food. When he couldn't go, I went. Then a rumor started that he was going to be arrested soon too."

That's when her husband decided to smuggle some documents to India. "The records were meant to inform the United Nations of the situation in the country. Nobody wanted to undertake such a dangerous mission, so my husband volunteered. They said, 'Not you, you have a wife and three children.' But he went anyway. Once he made it to India, he couldn't come back. Every day the Chinese came to ask where he was. In the end I decided to flee too. I pretended to go on a pilgrimage. It was one of the most difficult days of my life, because we had to leave my eldest daughter behind. I still cry when I think about that day. So as not to arouse suspicion, we hadn't told her anything. So my daughter went to school and when she came back, we had all disappeared. She also remembers this day as the hardest one in her life. Later on, other people brought her over to us."

From India she went to Canada and there the old woman joined the Women's Committee for a Free Tibet. The Tibetan women have an extensive network in the West. They organize discussion groups on the Internet, hold demonstrations and they lobby; but not about emancipation or women's issues. Every woman's conference, like the one in Beijing, is just a platform to talk about the fight for independence.

Feminist groups in the West have a theory about this. I hear this the same day, at the same conference. An American gives a lecture about the situation of Chinese women during the economic reforms. She says that it's typical that in every fight or conflict, whether it's a revolution, a war, or an economic change, the problems of women always come last. The leaders of these events, usually men, state that the struggle has to be won first. And women believe this and wait patiently. Once the fight is over, they discover that their leaders were never interested in their issues in the first place.

In the case of the Tibetan women, however, you can't blame the leaders. The Dalai Lama himself told the women to start an association. The women listened to their progressive Buddha and united in the TWA, but now they don't seem to know what to do with their organization. The women seem to think that they must wait until the Chinese leave and the new Tibet is born before they can start to address their own problems. By now, they have been waiting for 50 years.

PHURBU DOLMA, THE WOMEN'S ASSOCIATION SECRETARY

The secretary of the women's organization in McLeod speaks English fluently with a French accent. She grew up in France.

"You want my life story? But I'm not interesting. I never lived in Tibet. I don't know what it's like to flee over the mountains. I was born here, in India. My parents came from the same village as His Holiness. But I didn't know my parents until I was an adult; I only had a picture of them. I was in Europe. In the end, after a lot of work, I bought a ticket to India and then I met my parents and spent one month with them. That's why I always say that I've known my parents for a month.

"It's like this. When I was small, my parents sent me to the Tibetan Children's Village for orphans. I wasn't an orphan, but my parents had seven children. They had to live off a small salary and they weren't able to take care of all of us. So the TCV took me in. I was chosen to live in France. At that time there were so many children that the teachers tried to send some to Europe. Many went to Switzerland. We were a group of 20 children, ten boys and ten girls. There was a couple that served as our parents. I think this was in 1962. I was about six years old, but I don't know exactly how old I am or when my birthday is. My parents never registered that. I don't think it's a problem at all. I never need to lie about my age, or feel old.

"In France we started in kindergarten, because we first had to learn French. My foster parents were, as far as we were concerned, our real parents and the other children were our brothers and sisters. Except when you got into trouble and you were punished – then you started to fantasize about your real parents. We were a big group, so we didn't always get a lot of attention. The French government paid for our education and cost of living.

"We stayed there for ten years. Then, one summer, our foster parents told us to find a summer job, so we would be able to buy a plane ticket to India. I wasn't the only one; we all really wanted to see our families. I went to Switzerland and worked in a factory for a few weeks, cleaning windows. After that I worked in a village for handicapped people. Those patients had mental problems and we kept them company and played games with them. Everyone had one patient allocated to take for walks. The patients would be changed around, so it wouldn't become dangerous. I listened to their stories.

"After a few months, I had saved enough money for the trip and I went to Darjeeling. I had written to my parents to say that I was coming, so my mother was waiting for me with her friends. I couldn't find her, because she looked very different from the picture I had. My mother couldn't locate me either, but her friends recognized me; they thought I looked like her. Everybody started crying. It was so sad that a mother didn't recognize her own child.

"During my stay I asked my parents about everything, why they had sent me away. They told me that they got married late and then got one child every year, until there were seven. I was the middle child. They also told me that they didn't know my age, because they had so many children and their ages didn't matter to them.

"My parents had a difficult life. My mother worked as a housekeeper for a rich Tibetan family. My father was a cook, so he found a job in an Indian restaurant. Most men from Amdo can cook well. I always knew that they were poor. When I lived in France I sent them half of my pocket money. They never told me why they had fled Tibet. When I visited them, they were already old and frail. I do know that my father's Chinese was better than his Tibetan. But I didn't want to make my parents relive bad memories by asking them about their history.

"Once back in France I got married. My husband is from the group of children that I grew up with. We chose our own husbands, just like Westerners. But our foster parents did tell us that we should marry a Tibetan. They said that we were the seeds of the next generation and that we should spend our lives serving the Tibetan cause. They told us all the stories about Tibet. In the beginning, when we were small, we didn't really understand these tales. My foster parents would be talking about Lhasa, but we didn't know where that was. Of course we were friends with French children. Every year we would attend a summer camp and play with French kids our age. That's normal. But we did know where the limit was; we always felt like we were inbetween two cultures.

"We had a very simple wedding as we were young and didn't have money for a big feast. My parents had become sick by then, but I didn't know that. I had moved to Switzerland with my husband, and the letter had arrived in France, at the old address. By the time I received it, both of my parents had died. Luckily I was in time to do the pudja, a ritual you have to carry out within 49 days of someone's death.

"The deaths of my parents meant that I had to start sending money to my sister in India. She was married by then, had three children and had to take care of our younger brothers. For us, in Switzerland, money wasn't a problem. It was easy to get work there. We lived close to the Tibetan community and we did a lot of social work. Many newly arrived Tibetans didn't know the language, couldn't find a job and didn't know the laws. They were given all kinds of forms to fill out and they received letters from the government. Some couldn't even tell the difference between a letter and an advertisement, so we helped them. My husband was the leader of a group of boys from Lhasa, which raised money for the refugees in India.

"We had two children and an easy life there in Switzerland. We had jobs; we knew the country and the school facilities for the children were wonderful. But, through the social work we did, we also saw the dark side. There were many problems within the families of the Tibetans. Parents had to work hard, so they didn't have time for their children. The children didn't know their identities. There was a gap between the old and the new generation and there were many conflicts. Young people would get addicted to drugs and run away from home. We saw all these things happening and we decided that this wasn't the best way to live our lives. So we resolved to go back to India. Here, the children would go to a Tibetan school and learn the Tibetan identity. They would study Buddhism and Tibetan culture. I couldn't teach them those things, as I had grown up between two cultures myself. It would be much better if they discovered all these things themselves.

"At first we just sent my daughter to study here, as we weren't ready to move yet. That meant that we had to save money to visit her. My daughter was 12 then, which is a very sensitive age. Before she left, we bought her books about India and Dharamsala and we explained to her why we wanted her to go there. She is a very obedient child and so she accepted our wishes. We followed later. The first thing we did here was build a hotel. This was in 1989, and it was the right kind of enterprise for that time. After we had built ours, many other hotels followed. The guests are all Westerners; even then there were already many tourists.

"One day some women came to ask for a contribution to the Women's Association. I told them that I wasn't a member, but they said that every Tibetan woman was automatically an associate. At the time I was busy building the hotel. It was hard work because you had to go through a long administrative process. We had to learn to deal with the corruption here in India, and once the building was finished, we had to learn how to run a hotel. So I had my hands full. I asked them if I couldn't be a passive member instead of an active one, because I had no time. They agreed.

"But apparently they hadn't understood what a passive member was, because a year later they held elections and they chose me as the head of the bureau in Dharamsala. They came to see me and told me that I had been chosen for this post for three years and had to start working. I thought, 'What kind of place is this?' but since I didn't have a choice, I started.

"The most important thing about our association is that we exist. We were founded in 1959, while women were demonstrating in front of the Potala Palace in Lhasa. The people were very fearful, sitting there in front of the palace. So they started talking to each other, made a plan and set up an association. After the suppression of the protest, many leaders ended up in jail, and others were executed or disappeared. That way, the association died with them. The women who fled to India were not able to continue. There was a lot of confusion in the beginning. Everybody had to survive and nobody knew how long we would stay here. Now it's different. There is a government and the children have schools. But at that time, the women were in the dark.

"Then in 1984, His Holiness said during a meeting that he remembered that the women had an alliance and that it would be a good idea to start it up again. That's when they organized themselves. Now we have 39 departments. One of our goals is to find out what we want to do. We try to be the voice of the women in Tibet, so that they can be heard through us. And we want to show them how we feel. Apart from that, we do a lot of social work. We organize scholarships for children and we try to motivate girls to go to university. We do whatever needs to be done to help people.

"There wasn't a lot of discrimination against women in the old Tibet, especially not if you compare it to other countries. We didn't really have women's and men's tasks, everybody just helped to do the work that had to be done. I have heard that in some areas marriages were arranged and that some women married more than one husband. If the husband's brother didn't have a wife, she would take him on too. But that has nothing to do with discrimination, that was economic thinking. That way, the land would stay in the family. In other places in Tibet a man could marry two women. It just depended on which gender was in the minority. And they always had the right to refuse. If a woman didn't like her situation, she could divorce. It's true that there weren't many people who did that, because people in Tibet don't think about those things. They tend to just accept their circumstances. We are raised like that, you just adapt yourself. The young women in Tibet weren't educated either and since they were small, they had been prepared for their future life. It's like that. If you have learned to see problems, you are able to refuse things. But if you haven't, then you're just happy with the life you have. In any case, right now, the Chinese occupy Tibet, so we can't do anything to help the women.

"We all share the struggle for Tibet's independence and after that we will start to address feminist issues. Here in the community in Dharamsala, we don't really have problems either, so we concentrate on helping the elderly. We do encourage women to take the jobs that are necessary in society. We have, for instance, a lack of doctors, so we tell boys and girls to study medicine. There are always sick people everywhere. We also try to be democratic. His Holiness wants us to function as a democratic organization. That is not easy, you have to give the right training to your members, so we organize many workshops and meetings about human rights and democracy. We try to teach others how to deal with these issues. It's important, for later, when we'll have a real country."

14.

AN AUDIENCE WITH THE BUDDHA

The Dalai Lama has a round face and tiny eyes. He silently stares at me. I think back to a scene in *Kundun*, the Hollywood movie about his life. I saw it the day before on a shaky TV screen. In the movie, a Chinese messenger brings an official document that will force Tibet to become part of China. The young Dalai Lama sits on a high throne in his medieval Potala Palace in Lhasa. He wordlessly stares the Chinese official down.

The gaze is the same, even if the circumstances are not. Almost 50 years later, the Dalai Lama is seated in an upholstered chair in a Western villa in India. Opposite the iron gate of his house is his temple. Even that institution looks like an average house. Only when you come up the stairs do you see an enormous golden Buddha statue appear before you. Hundreds of Tibetan monks sit praying in front of it, dressed in their red robes. For them, the Dalai Lama is a Buddha and a king. He regularly leads them in prayer.

But life in exile changed their leader. The 'simple monk', as he likes to call himself, spent the last 50 years traveling the West looking for political support. He learned English and talks like a modern politician who knows his business. When home, he holds half-hour 'audiences' with journalists.

I'm lucky to be sitting in this room with him. When I arrived in Dharamsala, I didn't even know if he was in town. Communication between the Indian village and Beijing wasn't exactly straightforward. I sent faxes, but I had no idea whether they arrived, or who else read them on the way. In any case, there was never an answer. Then there is the Dalai Lama's schedule. The religious leader just got back from a trip to the United States, and a few days after my audience, he is on his way to Europe.

Other visitors and Tibetan followers can see him at the temple when there is a religious festival. One day, when I have an appointment with the secretary of the Dalai Lama, I walk onto the temple square. My bag is searched at the entrance. Everybody has to sit down on the ground in front of the leader's house. "He's coming!" someone whispers. "Who?" I ask stupidly. "His Holiness," the man informs me patiently. The first person to appear is an Indian soldier with a gun. The leader follows, a nice old man who stoops a little. Silence falls around the square. I feel like I'm watching a historical movie. A Western girl sits waving enthusiastically, but the Lama doesn't see her. He walks down the path, through the sitting Tibetans, and exchanges friendly words with an old woman. Two minutes later, he's gone.

To get an audience, I have to visit the secretary. He is a modern, friendly man in a polo shirt. We talk for 45 minutes about the future of Tibet, the optimism of the Tibetans. The secretary says many Tibetans see that the Chinese intellectuals are changing their attitude towards Tibet and they believe the Chinese authorities will follow this trend. The secretary complains about Westerners, like me, who just come to McLeod and think they can talk to the Dalai Lama. There's no way they could see their own state leaders without an appointment, he complains. Monday's audience is for people who applied six months ago. But he also has understanding for my situation. And so, two days later, I get my half hour after all.

Holding audiences turns out to be a non-stop affair. Before me, an Indian TV crew gets its 30 minutes, and afterwards there is a French journalist.

The Dalai Lama waits for me outside the reception room. "Dutch press," someone behind me says. I am immediately tongue-tied, so he leads me inside. The secretary is there too, this time in a traditional Tibetan coat. He sits ramrod-straight on a chair opposite us and behaves submissively. The Dalai Lama sits down and starts his staring session. While I introduce myself and my project (this book), he watches me silently. The first two questions I ask he answers with "Yes" and "Sure". Talk about a difficult beginning...

But after that, we have a nice conversation, much like the ones I have had with other Tibetans in the days before. Karma, my translator, was convinced that "after Monday" I would be a follower of "His Holiness." A Dutch colleague living in Delhi told me how his Dutch friends had come back in higher spirits from their audience with this impressive historical figure. So I'm waiting for this magical conversion. I try to feel the meaning of life, imagining that soon I'll be walking around in red robes, with a shaved head, praying to Buddha statues. Nothing happens. Maybe I'm too busy coming up with sufficiently original questions to receive a religious revelation. And of course, that's not why I'm in the reception room. We are there to talk about politics. And the Dalai Lama can do that just as professionally as he carries out his religious ceremonies. It's all in a day's work.

He doesn't regret anything, he says. "Let me think. My trip in 1954 to China was a good idea. The decision not to stay in India in 1957 was right, as was the choice to leave Lhasa in 1959. Here, in exile, I've built democracy and I took care that the youth gets well educated, all good policy. No, as far as I can see, I didn't make any major mistakes."

There is always the hope to go back to Tibet. "Of course! That day will come. I don't know when, but it could be possible within a few years."

I ask him what he expects from the new generation of Chinese leaders. He thinks it's too early to say anything about them. "The current government is a collective leadership and I'm not sure if that is good for us or not. When Deng Xiaoping was alive, you had the advantage of just having to talk to one person. He decided everything. During his lifetime, I really thought we would be able to find a solution. On the other hand, it's also good that there isn't just one strong leader in China. China's leaders now work under completely different circumstances to their predecessors. Even if they don't want to change, the situation in China has changed so much that they'll have to adjust. That also improves the chance that they'll deal with our problem in a more flexible way."

After all the criticism I have heard from the Tibetans about Western policy towards China, I ask the Dalai Lama which path he thinks Western countries should take. "China is a big country. We shouldn't isolate it, that wouldn't be good for anybody," the Tibetan leader replies. "I think the Chinese should become part of the international community as much as possible. And I also think that we need to negotiate with them on friendly terms. To totally isolate a country is one extreme. The other extreme is just wanting to do business with China, without caring about anything else. We shouldn't forget to put pressure on them about human rights and democracy. The West should be firm and clear on these issues. As long as Western countries try seriously to do something about the situation in China and Tibet, I think they're on the right track. But I see a dangerous trend of just looking at the big Chinese market, to trade, and to forget about human rights."

Negotiations between the Dalai Lama and the Chinese government have never led to any results. "I don't know if we will be able to have serious negotiations. We have tried many times in the past, but every time, China comes with new conditions. In fact they have never tried to have a real conversation. But I am always willing to talk, as soon as there is a positive sign from Beijing."

He laughs at the question whether time is on the side of the Tibetans or the Chinese. "Ha, ha. Half and half, I think. Every month that we wait, the damage that the Chinese do to Tibet increases. There is cultural genocide and the environment is destroyed. So in that way, our time is running out. If we wait much longer, there won't be anything left. On the other hand, the world and the international community is more and more aware of the situation in Tibet. And that becomes a growing problem for the Chinese government. They know they'll have to come up with a solution. The government is made to defend itself more and more. Even in its own country there are writers and artists who start to ask questions. The government can't go on giving excuses and making up lies. They will have to do something constructive eventually."

The religious leader does not let himself be influenced by the call for tougher actions by the Tibetan Youth Congress. "We have discussed a lot among the Tibetan community about which policy we should follow. We asked the people what they wanted: complete independence or my Middle Path, meaning more autonomy. We even collected some opinions from people in Tibet. And the majority of Tibetans inside and outside of Tibet still think that my Middle Path is the best. Of course they don't trust the Chinese, but the Tibetans in Tibet especially say that it is the most realistic policy."

Nonetheless, the religious leader has his doubts. This shows in his reaction to the hunger strikes. "The organizers of the hunger strike wrote me a letter, asking me not to come. I went anyway, because their battle is mine. I personally don't think these actions are the way, because I consider hunger strike and self-burning a form of violence. But I do understand their emotion. I gave them three statements to ponder: my great admiration for their sacrifice; the fact that I didn't agree with their way of protesting; and that, even though I didn't agree, I wouldn't ask them to stop their protest. During the eighties, I chose a clear policy with the peace plan that I presented in Geneva. I tried to negotiate for more autonomy, to be reached through peaceful means, and I gave up the idea of independence. But until now, this policy hasn't brought any results. It totally failed. That's why I didn't tell those people on hunger strike to stop. I would have to give them an alternative, and I don't have one."

I tell him about the Tibetans I met in China, who wait for him to come back so that he can take over the role of the Panchen Lama. But that is one thing the Dalai Lama is adamant about. "The Panchen Lama had a certain status in the Chinese government and had his responsibilities. I am not at all planning to take a political position. As soon as I go back to Tibet, I will give up my political leadership and will become a simple monk again. I know the Tibetan people trust me and love me. And until I die, I will do whatever I can for them. And not only for them, for anybody who needs help. But I see my future role more as one of spiritual and moral leadership. I want to improve human morals and tranquility. And I would be able to work to preserve Tibetan culture. But my people will follow me out of respect, not because of my position."

Does he think it would be unsafe for him to return? "Under the current circumstances it would be completely useless for me to go back. I'm not afraid of anything, but the local authorities in Tibet will try to use me as a marionette for their propaganda. During one of the last negotiations, the Chinese presented a five-point proposal. The points were all about me. I had to accept that Tibet had always been a historical part of China, I would get the same status and living circumstances as before my flight in 1959. But it isn't about me or my return. The issue here is the future of the Tibetan people. As long as the Chinese don't come with a serious resolution for the Tibetans, it's not time for me. We will have to work on establishing trust, because we won't get anywhere with all this mistrust."

But that is already a huge task. How do you ask trust from refugees who tell terrible stories about torture and aggression? "When you compare the Chinese communists to those of 20 years ago, the ones now have become more trustworthy. In those times, they would say something, and would do the opposite. Their policies changed all the time. Nowadays they are much more predictable and that makes negotiations and trust easier. Of course it is still difficult, but what else can you do? It's better to try than to give up beforehand. If we do that, we'll be sure to go nowhere."

Trust needs to be built not only between Tibetans and Chinese, but also between the Tibetans who left and the ones who stayed. But according to the Dalai Lama that shouldn't be an issue. "Oh yes, Redi, ha, ha. Those Tibetans act out of fear. I think you need to understand their circumstances. In another situation, they would say very different things. Somewhere deep inside they are still Tibetans."

He also says that he isn't against the communist doctrine. "I also had lessons in Marxism in those times, even if it wasn't entirely voluntary," he chuckles. "I found the theory very interesting. Here in India you also have people who studied Marxism, thought about it freely and became communists. That's the way it should be. The Chinese Communist Party made the crucial mistake of exaggerating the class struggle. Now there is a whole generation that has learned about communism by force. And that is not a conviction. Look at the current leaders. What's communist about them?"

After weeks in Dharamsala I stand, knees shaking, in front of a Chinese customs official. I'm trying to get back into China. My bag is filled with 'separatist material' which I need for this book, and in my passport there's a visa for India. The stamp now seems larger than life. I posted a picture of me with the Dalai Lama from Bangkok airport to Holland, along with a copy of my notes. You get scared, after spending days and days listening to stories of oppression and torture. I decide that if the Chinese authorities ask me what I did in India, I'm just going to tell the truth. I can already imagine the interrogation. In a special room here at the airport someone will explain the Chinese laws to me and force me to sign a statement. "If not," he'll threaten, "we will expel you." "I'm a journalist, and I'm just doing my job," is my imaginary reply and I demand a phone call to my husband and children, who are waiting for my arrival.

The customs official behind the counter looks up at me to see if I'm really the person in the passport picture, then types my name into his computer. I hold my breath. Then, with a face that shows only utter boredom, he bangs a big red entry stamp on top of my visa.

ENDNOTE

Musicians in Beijing

"I heard that you went to India and talked with the Dalai Lama," one of our Chinese friends asks innocently two weeks after my return. We are at a party on the outskirts of Beijing. All the guests are either musicians, painters, or both. They are sitting on pillows on the floor and are eating their supper from styrofoam containers. The artists have long hair, strangely shaped beards and they smoke a lot of cigarettes. Hovering over them are Western women, the objects of all their visual and musical art.

Surprised, I look at our friend. When you live in Beijing, you don't go around telling everyone that you interviewed the Dalai Lama. So my first question for him is how he knows where I went. The young man laughs, embarrassed, and says that my husband told him. He starts to bombard me with questions. He wants to know how I traveled to Dharamsala, and if I had contact with the exiles before I went. And what's the deal with the Dalai Lama anyway, does he want independence or not?

"I once went to Nepal and there were many Tibetans there too," he muses. "I thought it was strange, because those people were very successful merchants. They worked harder and earned much more money than the Nepalese. If they are such good businesspeople, how come Tibet is so poor?"

I answer that refugees all over the world tend to do better than the original inhabitants of whatever country they're in. They know that they're not in their own country and that they'll have to take care of themselves, that no one is going to help them. And as for Tibet, could the poverty there have been caused by China's disastrous policies? Deep in thought, my friend sips from his beer bottle and changes the subject.

My husband can't remember ever telling anybody about my meeting with the Dalai Lama, so he also doesn't understand how our friend could have known about my trip. Does the young musician work for the authorities? You never know. He wouldn't be the first of our friends to work for the Public Security Bureau. Those kinds of contacts make the life of a Chinese citizen much easier. Or does he belong to that group of writers and intellectuals that the Tibetans always talk about? The ones who ask questions about Tibet, not only among each other, but also to their leaders? Does he belong to that group of people on which the Dalai Lama has pinned all hope for the future?

We will never know, of course, but the best-case scenario would be if he were both.

ABOUT THE AUTHOR

After obtaining a degree in journalism, Annelie Rozeboom went to China for 12 months, and ended up staying 11 years. As the China correspondent for several national publications, she reported on the uprisings on Tiananmen Square, China's subsequent growth into an economic superpower, and the issue of Tibet. She now lives with her husband and their three children in Antananarivo, Madagascar, where she runs the only English-language newspaper in the country and teaches journalism and English at the American School of Antananarivo.

EXPLORE ASIA WITH BLACKSMITH BOOKS

From retailers around the world or from *www.blacksmithbooks.com*